Walking on Water

Walking on Water

ANTHONY DE MELLO

Translated by
PHILLIP BERRYMAN

A CROSSROAD BOOK
The Crossroad Publishing Company
New York

The Crossroad Publishing Company
16 Penn Plaza – 481 Eighth Avenue
New York, NY 10001

English translation copyright © 1998
by The Crossroad Publishing Company

Originally published by Edições Loyola, São Paulo, Brazil,
as *Caminhar sobre as águas* and *Quebre o 'idolo,* copyright © 1992

Printed in the United States of America

Library of Congress Cataloging-in-Publication Data
De Mello, Anthony, 1931 – 1987
    [Caminhar sobre as águas. English]
    Walking on water / Anthony De Mello; translated by
Phillip Berryman.
      p. cm.
    ISBN 0-8245-2492-6
    ISBN 0-8245-1737-7 (pbk.)
    1. Spiritual life – Catholic Church. 2. Catholic Church
–
Doctrines. I. Title.
BX2350.2.D38513 1998
248.4182 – dc21   97-47743
                                           CIP

1 2 3 4 5 6 7 8 9 10 13 12 11 10 09 08 07

Contents

Part One

*Prayer, love, spirituality, and religion
are about ridding yourself of illusions.
When religion brings that about, that's
wonderful, wonderful! When it deviates
from that, it is an illness, a plague to
be avoided. Once illusions have been
abandoned, the heart is unobstructed,
and love takes hold. That's when
happiness occurs. That's when change
takes place. And only then will you
know who God is...*

One

Vision

There is a wonderful line in the New Testament, where in speaking of love Paul says, "Love does not brood over injury." I sometimes tell people, "You're going to be disappointed when you get up there and discover that there is no sin that can't be forgiven by God." Once a woman who was supposedly having visions of God went to the bishop for advice. He told her: "You may be believing in illusions. You must understand, as bishop of the diocese, I am the one who can decide whether your visions are true or false."

"Yes, your excellency."

"That is my responsibility and my duty."

"Of course, your excellency."

"So you must do what I say."

"I will, your excellency."

"So listen: the next time God appears to you, as you say he appears, you are going to perform a test by which I will know if it really is God."

"Agreed, your excellency. But what is the test?"

"Say to God, 'Please tell me the personal and private sins of the bishop.' If it is God who is appearing to you, he will reveal my sins to you. Afterward come back here and tell me, but no one else. Okay?"

"I will, your excellency."

A month later, she asked to meet with the bishop, and he asked her, "Did God appear to you again?"

"I think so, your excellency."

"Did you ask him the question I told you to ask?"

"Of course, your excellency."

"What did God say?"

"God said to me, 'Go tell the bishop that I've forgotten all his sins!'"

What's this? No ledger where sins are recorded! Guess what — God does not keep any registry, any catalog. God sees us in the present and envelops us in a boundless love.

Two

Silence

This is a book about the means, a path for reaching God in our own time. I am going to be speaking about things like meditation, prayer, and other things intimately connected with prayer like love, joy, peace, life, freedom, and silence.

I want to begin with silence, and I'll tell you why: any route to God has to be a route toward silence. If you want to reach union with God someday, you must begin with silence.

What is silence?

In the East, a great king went to visit his spiritual master and said to him, "I am a very busy man. Could you tell me how I can reach union with God? But answer me in a single sentence."

And the master told him, "I am going to give you the answer in a single word!"

"What is that word?" asked the king.

The master said "Silence!"

"And how can I attain silence?" said the king.

"Meditation," said the master. In the East meditation means not thinking, beyond thought.

Then the king said, "And what is meditation?"

The master answered, "Silence!"

"How am I going to discover silence?"

"Meditation!"

"And what is meditation?"

"Silence!"

Silence means going beyond words and thoughts. What's wrong with words and thoughts? They are limited. God is not as we say God is, nothing that we imagine or think. That's what's wrong with words and thoughts. Most people remain trapped in the images they form of God. This is the greatest obstacle to reaching God. Would you like to experience the silence I am talking about?

The first step is understanding. Understanding what? Realizing that God has nothing to do with the idea I form of God.

In India there are many roses. Suppose I have never smelled a rose in my life. I ask what the aroma of a rose is. Could you describe it to me?

If we can't describe a simple thing like the fragrance of a rose, how are we going to be able to describe an experience of God? All words are inadequate. God is completely beyond words. That is what's wrong with words. A great mystic wrote a great Christian book called *The Cloud of Unknowing*. He said, "You want to know God?" There is only one way of knowing him: by unknowing! You have to get beyond your mind and your thought; then you will be able to perceive him with your heart. About God Thomas Aquinas says (and this is all that can be said with certainty): "We do not know what God is." That is also what the church says: "Any image that we make of God is more unlike God than like God."

If that is true, then what are the scriptures? Actually, they don't give us a portrait of God or even a description; they offer us a clue. For words cannot provide us with a portrait of God.

Suppose I am in my country, traveling toward Bombay. And I come to a sign that says "Bombay." I say, "Look, here's Bombay!" I look at the sign, turn around and start back.

When I arrive, people ask me, "Did you go to Bombay?"

"Yes, I did."

"And how is it there?"

"There's a sign there painted yellow with lettering, with a B, and so forth."

That sign isn't Bombay! Actually it doesn't even look like Bombay. It's not a picture of Bombay. It's a sign. That is what the scriptures are, a sign. "When the wise man points toward the moon, the only thing the fool sees is his finger."

Imagine that I am pointing toward the moon, and I say, "Moon." You come by and say, "Is that the moon?" and look at my finger. That is the danger and tragedy of words. Words are beautiful. "Father" — what a beautiful word to point to God. The church says that this is a mystery; God is a mystery. And if you take the word "Father" literally, you get stuck in problems because people are going to ask you, "What kind of a father is this who allows so much suffering?" God is a mystery! Unknown, unintelligible, beyond the mind!

Imagine a man born blind. He asks about the color green that everyone talks about. How would you describe it for him? Impossible. You listen to his questions, "Is it cold or hot? Big or little? Rough or smooth?" It's none of that. The poor man is asking out of his limited experiences.

Now suppose I were a musician and were to say, "I'm going to tell you how green is: It's like music." And then one day, the man gains sight and I ask him, "Have you seen green?"

He says, "No." Do you know why? He was looking for the music! He was so trapped in the idea of music, that even when he was looking at green, he couldn't recognize it.

～～ There is another story in the East about a little fish in the sea. Someone says to the fish, "Oh, how vast the ocean is. It is huge and marvelous!"

And the fish, swimming all over the place, asks, "Where's the ocean?"

"You're in it." But what he finds is water!

He doesn't recognize the ocean. He is trapped in the word. Might that be what is happening with us? Might it be that God is staring us in the face but because we're trapped in certain ideas we don't recognize God? That would be tragic!

Silence is the first step to reaching God and understanding that ideas about God are all inadequate. Most people are not ready to understand this, and that is a big obstacle to prayer.

Attaining silence involves becoming aware of the five senses, by using them. To many this may seem absurd and almost unbelievable, but all you have to do is look, listen, feel, smell, and see.

In the East we say, "God created the world. God dances in the world." Can you think of a dance without seeing the dancer? Are they a single thing? No. They're two, and God is in creation like the voice of a singer in a song. Let us suppose that I sing a song. You will have my voice and the song. They are intimately connected, but they are not the same thing. But think: Isn't it strange that we're listening to the song, not the voice? We see a dance and not the dancer?

Does that mean that we need only look and we will have the grace of seeing and recognizing God? No. You can receive the grace of seeing and recognizing. What is needed is a special way of looking.

The girl says something wonderful to the Little Prince, "It is only with the heart that one sees correctly. What is essential is invisible to the eyes." We must hear with the heart, see with the heart.

In a Japanese story, the disciple said to the master, "You are concealing the secret of contemplation from me."

The master said, "No, I'm not!"

The disciple replied, "Yes, you are!"

One day the two were walking alongside a mountain and heard a bird singing. The master said to the disciple, "Did you hear that bird sing?"

The disciple said, "Yes."

The master said, "Now you know I didn't hide anything from you."

The disciple said, "Yes."

Do you know what happened? He heard with the heart, he listened with the heart. This is a grace that we can be given if we look.

Imagine I'm looking at a sunset and a farmer comes up to me and says, "What are you looking at? You look ecstatic!"

I answer, "I'm ecstatic over Beauty."

The poor man begins to come every day in the afternoon looking for Beauty and asks where she is. He sees the sun, the clouds, the trees. But where is Beauty? He doesn't understand that Beauty is not a thing. Beauty is a way of seeing things. Look at creation! I hope that someday you will be given the gift of looking with the heart. But when you're looking at creation don't expect anything sensational.

Just look! Observe. Not the ideas — look at creation. I very much hope that this grace will be given to you, because you will be at peace when you see, and silence will take charge of you. Then you will be able to see. This is what Saint John's Gospel tells us so wonderfully, "All things were created in him and through him." And then that enchanting line that says, "He was in the world and the world was created through him, but the world did not recognize him." If you look perhaps you can recognize him. Look at the dance; I hope you will see the dancer.

~~~~ There is another instrument that I would like to recommend to you: sacred scripture. The scripture is the excellent portion, the finger pointed toward the Light. We use its words to go beyond conceptions and reach silence. How do you do that? Take a scripture passage, "On the last and greatest of the feast days, Jesus stood up and said in a loud voice, 'Let whoever is thirsty come to me and drink.' " Suppose that when you read it you are touched by Jesus' words. What are you to do? Recite this line in your heart (recite it — don't read it): "Let whoever is thirsty come to me and drink!" Repeat, repeat, until your heart is satisfied. There is no need to think about the meaning of the

words, because your heart knows the meaning. And when you get to this point of satisfaction, the words will react, will burst forth and some will say, "Whoever? Is that what you mean, God, anyone? Thief, sinner? Well here I am, give me to drink!"

Others, however, will react differently, saying, "I don't believe this. What drink are you talking about? I've come to you so many times in the past and you never gave me anything!" Here we have someone who is frustrated, and angry, for whom it is quite reasonable to talk to God in this manner. It is a great prayer, because it is presenting honestly what one has in one's heart. Yet someone else again may say, "I know exactly what you are telling me, Lord, because you have given me to drink! I'm back again and I'm thirsty."

It is a way of responding to being addressed by the Bible. But there may come a time when you are tired of reacting with words, when feelings swelling in your heart may be so deep and rich that no word is capable of expressing them. The only thing you will be able to do will be to do nothing, in silence. Respond to those words and to God beyond any word that you could use. And remain in silence as long as you are not distracted. When you become distracted, pick up the Bible and keep reading until you are touched by another line.

This is one way to use the words of scripture to go beyond them, to silence. Read, recite, and respond. Soon the reaction will be silence. And in silence you will find God.

There is another way to use scripture. You remain in silence, looking and listening.

That will lead you to silence. And when you reach this deep tranquility, recall a line from the Bible.

Do you know what will happen? The words of scripture will seem etched in your heart. They will have such a strong meaning that it will deepen the silence. They have a meaning beyond the mind. Could these words disturb your silence? No! It is like the peace and quiet of evening, and you hear a bird or the tolling of a church bell and these sounds deepen your silence. This is what will happen to you if you remain in silence and someone reads a line from scripture or if you recall one.

Think about these statements of Jesus:

—"Come, follow me!"

—"All is possible to one who believes. Do you believe that I can do this?"

—"Peace!"

—"Fear not, it is I!"

—"Do you love me?"

Imagine that Jesus Christ is here, right in front of you, and that he addresses these words to you. You have to resist the temptation to answer. Don't say anything, don't answer. Let the words reverberate in your heart, let them enwrap your whole being. And when you can contain yourself no longer, react, give your response. It is very likely that you will enter into silence long before giving the response. This is a very simple and efficient method for attaining silence. Use it.

Imagine that Jesus is standing right in front of you and is addressing to you one of these gospel expressions that are so full of love. Hold back your reaction, and when you can do so no longer, speak to him.

Now I want to tell you a story which sums up the spirituality of looking and listening. A story is the shortest distance between a human being and truth.

～～ There was a temple built on the edge of an island, around two miles offshore. That's where the island was. And in the temple were a thousand silver bells, large and small. Bells made by the best artisans in the world. And whenever the wind blew or a storm arose, the bells chimed. It was said that whoever heard those bells would be enlightened and led into a deep experience of God. The centuries went on, and gradually the temple (and the bells) sank into the sea. But the traditional belief continued to be that from time to time the bells chimed and whoever had the gift of hearing them would be transported to God.

Attracted by the legend, a young man set out on a journey of many miles until he stood looking

out over the place where it was said that the temp
had stood many years before. He sat down in the
first shade he found and began to try to hear the
sound of those bells.

Try as he might, the only thing he managed to
hear was the noise of the waves breaking on the
beach or crashing against the rocks. That annoyed
him because he was trying to block out that noise
so he could hear the bells toll. And so he strove for
a week, four weeks, eight weeks … three months
went by. When he was about to give up, he heard
the elders of the village at night speaking about
the tradition and about the people who received
the grace, and his heart was on fire. But he knew
that a heart aflame was no substitute for the sound
of those bells. After trying for six or eight months,
he decided to give up. Perhaps it was just a legend;
perhaps the grace was not for him.

He said goodbye to the people living there
and went to the beach to say goodbye to the tree
that had offered him shade, and to the sea and
the sky. While he was there he began to listen
to the sound of the waves and discovered for

the first time that it was a pleasing and relaxing sound; and the sound led him to *silence*. And as the silence deepened, something happened. He heard the ringing of a tiny bell. He was overwhelmed and thought, "I must be producing that sound; it must be the power of suggestion!" Once more he began to listen to the sound of the sea; he relaxed and remained in silence. The silence became more intense, and again he heard the ringing of a tiny bell. Before he could even be surprised, another bell rang, and then another and another and another and others ... And then a symphony of a thousand temple bells was ringing in unison. He was transported out of himself and received the grace of union with God.

~~~ If you want to hear the sound of a bell, listen to the sound of the sea. If you want to recognize the dancer, look at the dance. If you want to hear the voice of a singer, listen to the song. Look, listen, experience what some day will be granted to you to recognize within you.

Three

Peace

There were two monks who lived together for forty years and never argued. Not even once. One day, one said to the other, "Don't you think it's time we had an argument, at least once?"

The other monk said, "Fine, let's start! What shall we argue about?"

"How about this piece of bread?" said the first monk.

"Okay, let's argue about this bread. How are we going to do it?" said the second.

The first said, "This bread is mine; it belongs to me."

The second said, "If it is, take it."

Peace isn't necessarily destroyed by a quarrel or an argument. It is the "I" that destroys peace. This is mine, and I don't want to split it with anyone. When you take such an attitude of attachment and selfishness, your heart gradually becomes harder and harder. This is the great enemy of peace: a heart that is attached, hardened, and selfish.

Imagine a nation where one group of people has vast lands and money and says, "We're not going to divide our wealth with anyone." Imagine that in the United Nations every nation were to take this position, "We're concerned only about our own welfare, and we have little concern for anyone else." How could there be peace in a situation like that? Hardened hearts, hardened nations. But before talking about nations, let's talk about you and me.

Look at your own heart. You could say, "There are so many arguments and quarrels in my life!"

And I say, "But there is no resentment, bitterness, or hatred."

You say, "There is so much pain and suffering in my life!"

And I say, "But your conscience is not disturbed."

You say, "There is a great deal of activity and action in my life."

And I say, "But no upset nerves or tension."

Can you say this? If you can, you will be builders of peace in this vast world. And the very purpose of prayer is to spread peace everywhere. How is that done? Are we going to do it? Are we going to do it now?

Close your eyes. You are going to do a very simple spiritual exercise that is not going to last more than a minute or two. Close your eyes and get in contact with your body. Be alert to the contact of clothing with your shoulders, the clothing touching your back. Your hand. Feel your hand resting on something or your hands touching each other. Feel your buttocks weighing down on the chair. Your feet touching your shoes or the floor. Again: shoulders, back, hands, buttocks, feet. Again, slowly: shoulders, back, hands, buttocks, and feet. Now gently open your eyes. The exercise is over.

What happened when you did the exercise I proposed? Did you feel relaxed or tense? Most people feel relaxed; few feel tense. If you are one of those who did feel tense, I suggest that you get in touch with the tension. Where in your body do you feel the tension? Remain as alert to the tension as possible. You will gradually relax.

If you do this exercise for five or ten minutes, you will begin to feel sleepy and will even fall asleep, from being so relaxed.

Does this relaxation exercise bring the peace I am talking about? This isn't a relaxation exercise; it's an attention exercise. Fine, but did it bring peace? Yes, it brought peace — hard as that might be to believe. You know what happens when you do this exercise? It is as though you entered into yourself. It is as if you felt all kinds of things, experienced things, saw amazing things.

~~~ One day God got tired of people. They were always pestering him, asking for things. So he said, "I'm going away to hide for a while." So he gathered all his advisers and said, "Where should I hide? Where's the best place for me to hide?"

Some said, "Hide on the highest mountain peak on earth."

Others said, "No, hide at the bottom of the sea; they'd never find you there."

Others, "Hide on the other side of the moon; that's the best place. How are they going to find you there?"

Then God turned to his most intelligent angel and asked him, "Where do you advise me to hide?"

The intelligent angel smiled and said, "Go hide yourself in the human heart. That's the only place where they never go!" A beautiful Hindu story! What it says is very contemporary. You know that simple attention exercise I proposed? It takes you to your heart. It takes you back home. This is what it means to turn to the heart. You go back home, you return to yourself, and in a very simple way. All you have to do is get in touch with your body. But you have to do it for yourself. If you are consistent, over time you will discover a whole series of mysterious things that will bring peace; your heart will be at peace and your fears will disappear. But this takes time. There is no instant formula for peace. It has to be sought calmly.

You may say that time is just what you don't have. But let's suppose that you're driving a car. Feel the steering wheel in your hands, feel the seat, feel your feet touching your shoes, get in touch with your body. Don't close your eyes! Feel the movement of your body when you are walking. That will calm you, and I hope you discover something of what these exercises can give.

And you will be motivated enough to try to do the exercise, to really sit and get in touch with the feelings of your body. Beginning at the top of your head, observe all your body's feelings. Face, neck, chest, and so forth down to the tip of your toes. Then begin again, from the top of your head down. That's how it's done.

Let me mention some of the effects of these exercises, even though it is almost always impossible to talk about them. "Do it and you will see!" is what they say in the East. But what should happen with someone who does this exercise? The first thing: you're going to become alive, you're going to be in the present. And that is something wonderful. To be able to really be in the present! You never remember where you put things? You're always tense, on the brink of exhaustion? You can't concentrate? You don't remember anything? These are symptoms that you need to live in the present.

A great guru in the East was talking to a group of executives, and he said, "Just as a fish dies on dry land, you will die if you remain stuck in the matters of the world. The fish has to return to the water, and that's where it really lives. You have to return to your own heart!"

Then the executives said, "You mean we have to give up our businesses and enter a monastery?"

"No, no," said the guru. "I didn't say enter a monastery. Continue your businesses and turn to your heart."

Do you see? Turning to the heart doesn't mean entering into some mysterious kind of mystical fantasy. It means coming back home, to your self; it means coming back to the present. From then on you will live.

There is something else that these exercises provide: they will help you to be calm, and you will slow down. Speed is a wonderful thing; I don't have anything against it. But when speed becomes haste, it's a poison.

The Japanese have a saying that we ought to heed: "The day you stop traveling, you will arrive."

And I would say, "The day you stop running, you will arrive."

That reminds me of a father who was with his children in a museum and he was saying, "Hurry, hurry, because if you stop to look at each thing, you won't see anything!" This is what is so terrible in life. This is what all of us are doing. We go through our whole life trying to save time, and we are losing our very life. You know what I mean? It is as Jesus said, "You've gained the world and lost your soul!"

I remember a young man who was traveling with his wife. He was crazy about speed. His wife got out the map and said, "Dear, we're on the wrong street!" And he said, "It doesn't matter, we're breaking a record." There you have what's terrible about modern life. That may be what many of us are doing. But do you know what the exercise that I offered will do for you? It will slow you down.

How much time does it take you to get to work? Twenty minutes? Start taking twenty-one. I know that some people must think I'm nutty, but take twenty-one! How much time do you spend drinking coffee? Ten minutes? Spend eleven on it! You will benefit with the few seconds you add to each thing you do. In a week you will begin to be in the present.

An Indian, a businessman, told me he was quite afraid of taking up meditation out of fear that his business dealings would suffer. I told him the exercises that I am offering are precisely for busy, active people. They're not for some reclusive mystic far removed from all this! The businessman still hesitated, but then finally gave in—and when he practiced the exercises that I am recommending to you, his businesses tripled.

He was more relaxed, more concentrated. He shifted to doing one thing at a time. That is the great benefit of prayer: concentration. You start doing one thing at a time, and you are completely present to each act you undertake.

It's easy to understand why that man's businesses improved, and why he became so much more efficient.

Are these exercises spiritual? Is this meditation? I say yes. There are millions of people in the East who do only this, nothing more, and they attain a high spirituality. That is the key point of prayer: God and spirituality must be found in life. Not outside it. You remember when I was talking about silence? The same is true here.

And prayer? It all depends on how you define it. If by prayer you understand conversation with God, no, this isn't prayer because you're not conversing with God while you're paying attention to the feelings of your body, to your body's movement when you walk. But if by prayer you understand union with God, then it really is prayer. You will come to understand prayer through that simple exercise that I have given you: paying attention to the feelings in your body.

~~~ There are many other benefits that this exercise will bring: spiritual blessings, acceptance, for example. But you will discover that for yourselves. Suppose some of you don't have patience and perseverance to keep doing this exercise. In that case, I recommend two other simple spiritual exercises. The first is an acceptance exercise, "Lord give me the grace to change what can be changed, to accept what can't be, and

wisdom to know the difference." There are so many things in our lives that can't be changed! We are powerless, and if we learn to say yes to these things, we will reach peace. Peace is in the yes. You can't stop the clock; you can't prevent the death of a loved one; you can't change the limitations of your body and your inabilities.

So place yourself before the things you can't change. And say yes. In doing that, you will be saying it to God. Of course it's hard. Don't strain. But if you can say yes in your heart, you will be saying yes to God's will.

By sticking with this attitude you will have peace even in the things that you are struggling to change.

~~~ The second supplementary exercise is one of detachment: think about your childhood, when you yearned for something so tenaciously that you couldn't stop thinking about it. You couldn't live without it. Think about something you detested and hated when you were a child

or about some of the things you were afraid
Many of these fears and longings are now gone.
What happened to them? They've gone away,
right? The exercise is as follows: make a list of the
things on which you are dependent, the things
of which you feel in charge, the things you don't
want to be deprived of. And say to each one of
them, "All this will pass away." Make a list of
unpleasant things that you can't stand, and say to
each of them, "This too will pass away."

When Jesus was born the angels sang of peace,
and when he died he left us a present: his peace.
"I leave you my peace." Peace is a gift; we can't
produce it, let alone create it. All that we can do
is dispose our hearts to receive it. Remember that
Syrian general who went to the prophet in Israel to
be cured of leprosy and the poet said, "Go bathe
in the Jordan River seven times"?

The man was angry and said, "Don't we have
better rivers in my country? And I have to bathe
here in the Jordan River? I thought this prophet
was going to lay his hands on me and cure me!"

One of the servants said to the general, "Sir, if the prophet had told you to do something difficult, you would have done it! But he asked you for something easy and simple." Try these simple easy exercises. You won't believe the effects that they will have on you. But when you experience the effects you won't have to believe any more.

Four

Happiness

One of the most quoted lines in Christian literature is that of Augustine, "Our hearts were created for You, O Lord, and they will be restless until they rest in You." Whenever I hear this line, I am reminded of another line made famous by one of our greatest mystical poets in India, Kabir. He wrote a beautiful poem that begins with the following line, "I laughed when they told me that a fish in the water is thirsty." Settle on this image: a thirsty fish in the water! How can it be? We human beings enwrapped in God being restless! Look at creation: trees, birds, grass, animals…All creation is full of joy. All creation is happy! I know there is suffering, pain, growth, decline, old age, and death. All this is in creation, but we must understand what happiness means! Only the human being is thirsty, only the human heart is restless.

Isn't that strange? Why is the human being unhappy, and what can be done to change that unhappiness into happiness? Why are people so sad? Because they have mistaken ideas and wrong attitudes.

The first mistaken idea that people have is that happiness means euphoria, sensations of pleasure, fun. On the basis of that idea, people go looking for intoxicants and stimulants and end up depressed. The only thing with which we ought to intoxicate ourselves is life. It is a calm sort of intoxicant but one that is lasting. This is the first mistaken idea from which we ought to free ourselves. Happiness doesn't mean being euphoric—not necessarily.

The second mistaken idea is to think that we can pursue our own happiness, that we can do something to attain it. I am almost contradicting myself, because later I'm going to say what we can do to reach happiness, but happiness cannot be sought in itself. Happiness is always a consequence.

The third and perhaps most decisive idea about happiness is that it is always found in the outside, in external things, in other persons. "By changing my job, perhaps I will be happy," or who knows, "Changing where I live, marrying someone else, I will be happy," etc. Happiness has nothing to do with the outside. Money, power, respectability promise to bring happiness. But they don't. Poor people can be happy.

〜〜 I recall the story of a prisoner held by the Nazis. The poor man was tortured every day. One day they changed his cell. In the new cell there was a skylight through which he could see a patch of blue sky during the day and some stars at night. The man was overjoyed, and he wrote to his family members about this good fortune. When I read this story, I looked at my door. I had the vast expanse of nature to appreciate. I was free, I wasn't a prisoner, I could go wherever I wanted! Yet I think I had only a fraction of the joy of that poor prisoner.

I remember reading a novel about a prisoner in a Soviet concentration camp in Siberia. The poor man was awakened at four in the morning and given a piece of bread. He thought, "It's better for me to hold onto a little of this bread, because I may need it at night. I'm so hungry I can't sleep. If I eat at night, maybe I'll sleep." After working all day, he lay down in bed, pulled up the blanket that hardly kept him warm, and thought, "Today has been a good day. Today I didn't have to work out in the freezing wind. And tonight, if I wake up hungry I have a piece of bread with me, and so I'll eat it and sleep well." Joy, happiness! Do you believe it?

I once met a woman who was paralyzed. Everyone would ask her, "Where do you get this happiness that shines through you all the time?"

"I have all the most marvelous things in life. I can do the most beautiful things in life." Paralyzed in the hospital and full of happiness—what an extraordinary woman!

Happiness is not found on the outside. Get rid of that mistaken notion or you'll never find happiness.

There's something else that you have to disabuse yourselves of if you want to find happiness and joy. We have to change some of our attitudes. Which ones? The first is the attitude of a self-centered child. Have you ever seen a child saying, "If you don't play with me, I'm going home"?

Look at yourselves. Think about what causes you unhappiness and see if you can detect this line that you say almost unconsciously, "If they don't give me this or that, I won't be happy." "If I don't get this or that doesn't happen, I won't be happy." Many persons aren't happy because they are imposing conditions on their happiness. Discover whether this attitude exists in your heart and if it does, get rid of it.

There is a fine story about a man who was always begging for all kinds of things from God. One day, God looked at him and said, "I'm fed up! Three requests, and that's it. I'll answer these three petitions, and then I'm not going to give anything more. State your three wishes!"

The man was enchanted and said, "I can ask anything?"

And God said, "Yes! Three requests and no more!"

And the man said, "Lord, you know, I'm ashamed to say, but I would like to get rid of my wife because she's an old bag and is always...Lord, you know. She's unbearable! I can't live with her. Could you rid me of her?"

"Fine," said God, "let your wish be fulfilled." And his wife died.

The man felt guilty because of the relief that he felt, but he was happy and relieved and thought, "I'm going to get married to a more attractive woman." When the relatives and friends came to the funeral and began to pray for the dead woman, the man suddenly changed his mind, and exclaimed, "My God, I had this wonderful wife. I didn't appreciate her while she was alive." Then

Happiness

There's the story of a man who one day ran to his rabbi and said, "Rabbi, you have to help me! My house is hell! We live in one room, my wife, my children, my in-laws, and me. It's hell! There's not enough room for all of us."

The rabbi smiled and said, "Okay, I'll help you, but you have to promise to do whatever I say."

And the man said, "I promise, I really promise! It's a solemn promise!"

The rabbi said, "How many animals do you have?"

The man said, "A cow, a goat, and six chickens."

The rabbi said, "Put the animals in the room and come back in a week." The man did not believe what he was hearing, but he had promised. Then he went back home depressed and brought the animals into the room. The next week, he went back discouraged and said to the rabbi, "I'm going crazy! I'm going to end up having a stroke. You have to do something..."

And the rabbi said, "Go back home and put the animals outside. Come back to see me in a week." The man went running back to his house. And when he came back the next week, his eyes were shining, and he said, "Rabbi, the house is a wonder, so clean. It's paradise!"

Get it? "I didn't have any shoes and I was always complaining about not having shoes, until I met someone who had no feet!"

Think about that extraordinary woman Helen Keller. Unable to hear, speak, or see and yet so overflowing with life. If you can be grateful, you will find the secret of happiness. Try it.

Put yourself in the place of that paralyzed woman that I was telling you about before. Put yourself in her place! You could even lie down on the ground in order to better feel what it's like. Imagine that you are paralyzed and say, "I can do all the most beautiful things in the world! I have the most beautiful things in the world." And you will find love, taste, smell, sight, sound. You will go on to hear the birds singing, the breeze in the trees, and the voices of your friends; you will see their faces. You will discover all these things and will be able to savor the secret of gratitude.

There's another exercise you can practice. It is very simple: think about the previous day. Remember everything that happened yesterday, one after another, and for all the events say, "Thank you!" "How lucky I was that this happened to me!" You will probably also recall something unpleasant. Stop at that point. Think, "This thing that happened to me was put there for my good." Think like that, say thank you, and move on.

The two previous exercises were about gratitude. The last exercise is about faith, faith that everything is given, allowed by God, for the good of each one of us.

I call this exercise "blessing." Think about events in the past whether pleasant or not. And say, "They were good for me; they were good!" Think about the things that are happening to you and say, "It's good, it's good…" Think about the future and say, "It's going to be good, it's going to be good…" And see what will happen. Faith will become happiness. Faith that everything is in God's hands and that everything will redound to our happiness.

There is a story about a man who runs out to meet a monk who is passing by the village. "Give me the stone," he cries, "the precious stone!"

The monk says, "What stone are you talking about?"

The man says, "Last night God appeared to me in a dream and said, 'A monk will be passing by the village at noon tomorrow, and if he gives you a rock that he is carrying with him, you will be the richest man in the country.' So give me the stone!"

The monk reached into his sack and took out a diamond; the biggest diamond in the world, the size of a human head! And he said, "Is this the stone you want? I found it in the forest. Take it!" The man seized the stone and went running home. But he couldn't sleep that night. Very early the next morning he went to where the monk was sleeping under a tree, woke him up, and said, "Here's your diamond back. I want the kind of wealth that enables you to throw wealth away." That is what we have to discover if we want to find happiness.

Five

Life

One day Buddha was sitting with all his disciples around him when an old man appeared and said, "How long do you want to live? Ask for a million years and they will be granted to you!"

Buddha answered without hesitation, "Eight years!"

When the old man was gone, his disciples disappointedly pressed him, "Master, why didn't you ask for a million years? Think of the good that you would do for hundreds of generations!"

And the old man replied with a smile, "If I were to live a million years, people would be more interested in extending their lives than in seeking wisdom."

Do you know what he meant? That they were more interested in surviving than in improving the quality of their lives. How true that is! Few spend time and energy to improve the quality of their existence. You can live without having lived. People think they are alive because they are breathing, eating, speaking, conversing, and going from one place to another. They're not dead of course. But are they really alive? What does it mean to really be alive? It means three things: being yourself, being now, and being here.

Being alive means being yourself. To the degree that you are you, you are alive. We might ask, "I'm not myself? Who would I be if not myself?" It's quite possible that you are not yourself, that you are a puppet.

Suppose you have a puppy. We insert a radio receiver in its brain and we send it to the other side of the world, let's say to China. And from here we keep sending it signals. We say, "Stand up," and the puppy gets up. "Sit," and the puppy sits. "Lie down," and the puppy lies down. And everyone is astonished, "What is happening with this puppy?" It's under remote control. That is a very appropriate image for millions of people.

People come to consult me about their spiritual and emotional problems, and I often find myself asking, "What are the voices that these people's voices are responding to? What voices from the past?" And I keep finding people who are worried, depressed, full of prejudices.

Einstein said it was easier to split an atom than a prejudice. People are not themselves by any means; they are controlled. They become puppets; their behavior, feelings, and attitudes are mechanical. They don't have living feelings, or living behavior, and don't know it. They are responding to the voices of persons from the past and to experiences from the past. They've had some experiences that affected them, that control them, and consequently they aren't free, they aren't alive. That is the greatest obstacle to the spiritual life.

"If you would be my disciples, you have to hate father and mother!" People are shocked at Jesus. What does that mean? Jesus certainly did not mean that we have to hate our parents. No! We have to love them as we love all human beings.

The father and mother Jesus is talking about are the Father and Mother that we carry in our minds and that control us. Those voices! This is what we have to free ourselves from, tear out of ourselves. When we stop living mechanically, we will stop being puppets. How will we be able to have a spiritual life if we aren't alive? How be disciples of Jesus, if we are mechanical, puppets?

It is a basic question: How to stop being mechanical? There is an exercise that can help us in this regard. It looks easy but it isn't, and if you persist, you will see the difference.

Here is the exercise: think of some event from the recent past, something that happened yesterday or in the past week. Don't shy away from recalling an unpleasant event. If it was unpleasant, so much the better. You must observe your reaction to your recollections. How are you reacting emotionally? What kind of convictions and attitudes do you have about this event? Just observe and ask yourself what voice you are responding to. Have the courage to ask, "Might this not be the reaction of someone else reacting inside me? Someone from the past that I am carrying around?" This exercise lasts a few seconds, no more than a minute. If you want to attain all its effects, you will have to delay more, and observe various events in the day. Look at your reactions. Look, don't judge, don't condemn, don't approve; be an impartial observer. Look! You don't even have to ask the questions that I suggested. If that distracts you, don't ask. Just look. The machinery will disappear, life will begin to enter in, and you will notice the difference.

I know an extraordinary man who is paralyzed. He told me, "You know, Father, I really began to live after I was left paralyzed. For the first time in my life, I had time to look at myself, see my life, my reactions and thoughts. My life became much deeper, richer, and more attractive than before." Isn't it striking that someone paralyzed has found life and that so many people freely moving around from one place to another haven't found it, because they are paralyzed inside?

This is the big obstacle: lack of time! Everyone tells me they have no time. "Where am I going to find time to do that?" What are you spending your time on? Keeping up this mechanical life? I'm reminded of the robber who said to a man, "Your money or your life!" And the man said, "Okay, y-you'd b-better take my life, because I need money for my old age!" It would be funny if it weren't so tragic.

Observe your reactions to each thing that happens during the day; observe your convictions. Raise questions! Are you open to questioning your convictions? If you're not, you're prejudiced and mechanical.

I recall a brilliant young rabbi, who succeeded his equally brilliant father, also a rabbi. People said to him, "Rabbi, you are completely different from your father!" And the young man laughed, "I'm just like my father! My father didn't imitate anyone, and I don't imitate anyone. He wasn't a carbon copy, and neither am I." That is what being alive means, being unique. Get rid of those voices and that remote control.

~~~ There's a second thing that you need to be alive: being now. What does that mean? It means, first, understanding something that very few people understand: that the past is unreal, that the future is unreal, and that living in the past or in the future means being dead. I know that there are wonderful things from the past, that we can learn lessons from it, that the past has influenced us and shaped us, and so forth. Great! But it's not real! We do have to plan the future. Actually, if you hadn't planned the future, it's very likely that you wouldn't be listening to me now. But the future isn't real; it's a notion in our head. And to the extent that you're living in the future or in the past, you're not now, you're not here.

A family is going to take a three-day trip to Switzerland. They spend months planning their vacation, and when they get there, they spend most of the time planning their trip back. While they're in Switzerland, instead of enjoying that astonishing scenery, instead of breathing the air, they are busy taking photos to show their friends. Photos of places that they've never been. They were there physically, but they weren't really there, they were somewhere else. Unreal vacation, unreal life! We live in a future culture—the culture of tomorrow. Tomorrow I'm going to be happy; tomorrow I'm going to live. And so, when I get to high school, I'm going to live; when I'm in the university, I'm going to live. And when you get to the university, you'll say, "When I get married, I'm going to live." After you get married, "Okay, when the children grow up, I'm going to live." When the children grow up, you're not going to know what it means to live! You're very likely to die without having lived.

Are you ready for a shock? Listen! Examine your own life. Look at all your thoughts, and you will see how often they are in the past or in the future. Seeing how little you live in the present, how little alive you are, is a shock. Think about it this way: you are peeling an orange to eat it. If your mind is completely focused only on eating the orange, you won't be peeling the orange because you won't be there, and when you're eating that orange, you won't be tasting it, because you'll be somewhere else.

A wise old boatman was taking pilgrims to a shrine. One day someone asked him, "Have you been to the shrine?" "No, not yet," said the boatman, "because I still haven't discovered everything the river has to offer me. In this river I find wisdom; I find peace; I find God." But the pilgrims didn't even notice the river; their minds were so focused on the shrine they couldn't see the river. Could that be the story of our lives? It's like washing the cup to drink coffee without really washing the cup, because we're not there, and never drinking the coffee, because we're not there, and so forth. That is a tragedy. Our life slips away!

What is the cure for this? A legend says that Buddha traveled all over the country seeking enlightenment; he went to the greatest masters of his time, and he practiced all the disciplines and spiritualities that existed, but enlightenment didn't come. Finally he quit. In desperation, he sat under a fig tree and was enlightened. Years later, his disciples asked him, "Master, tell us the secret of enlightenment. How do we attain it?" There is no secret, no technique. The old man tried to explain that. But his disciples wanted the technique.

Then Buddha — I imagine him winking — said, "All right, I'm going to give you a technique. When you are inhaling, be aware that you are inhaling. And when you are exhaling, be aware that you are exhaling." Isn't that marvelous? It doesn't seem very spiritual. Do you know what he intended? He wanted his disciples to come into the present! He knew, enlightened as he was, that God isn't tomorrow; God is now. Life isn't tomorrow; it's now. Love isn't tomorrow; it's now. Enlightenment is now. If you come into the present, it can happen. Yes, it can happen.

This is very similar to the exercise for achieving peace. "Do some everyday thing, and as you do it, verbalize what you are doing." This is a very good exercise for entering into the present, for coming to the here and now and to life. This is

the second thing you have to do to be alive. To be yourselves, be now.

〰〰 We are going to look at the third thing: being here. This means getting out of your head and returning to your senses, literally. Leaving abstraction behind and entering into experience.

There is a story of an American soldier in the Korean war. He was very homesick on Thanksgiving Day, and a couple that had lived many years in the United States invited him for supper that day. When the soldier arrived, to his great surprise and joy, he saw that they were having turkey, his favorite dish. Then he took a generous serving, and as soon as the meal began he started to have a discussion with his host. When the discussion was over, the meal also ended. The soldier saw that he had not enjoyed the meal, that he had not even tasted the turkey. He had not entered into the "here."

Arguments are wonderful, and so are ideas. But ideas aren't life! They are excellent for guiding

us in life. But they aren't life. Abstraction isn't life. Life is found in experience. It is like reading a wonderful menu. You can guide your lives by the menu, but the menu isn't the meal. And if you spend all your time with the menu, you're never going to eat anything. Sometimes it's even worse. There are people who are eating the menu. They are living off ideas, letting life slip away.

What are we to do to overcome this? Krishnamurti warns us, "The day we teach a child the name of a bird, the child stops seeing the bird." The child looks at that sprightly thing, full of mystery and surprise, and we teach it: it's a sparrow. The child now has an idea: sparrow. And later, whenever it sees a sparrow, it's going to say, "Well, you know, it's a sparrow…" The same thing applies to the idea, let us suppose, of an American. Every time I see an American citizen go by I say, "American." And I miss out on the unique being that this individual is. Have you experienced seeing a child in wonder looking at this mysterious trembling vibrant thing that we call a sparrow? The idea, the word, can be an obstacle to seeing the

sparrow. The word "American" can be an obstacle keeping me from really seeing the American in front of me. The word and idea "God" can be an obstacle to seeing God.

How resolve this? You can do it right now. Listen to all the sounds that you can detect around you. Can you hear all of them? Are there loud sounds, soft sounds, the sound of a voice? You enter into your senses and that's where experience lies. There's no abstraction there, no idea. Look at what you're seeing, listen to what you're hearing, touch what you're touching, feel what you're feeling.

There is a famous guru who became enlightened. His followers asked him, "Master, what did you get out of your enlightenment? What has enlightenment given you?"

The man answered, "Well, I'm going to tell you what it has given me: when I eat, I eat; when I look, I look; when I listen, I listen. That is what I have been given!"

His followers replied, "But everyone does that!" And the master laughed heartily, "Everyone does that? Then everyone must be enlightened!" The point is that almost nobody does that, almost nobody is here, alive.

~~~ Being alive means being yourself, being alive means being now, and being alive means being here. Look at yourself. To the degree that you can observe yourself, not just mentally, but as an impartial observer, you will put aside your mechanical and puppet existence and will come to be a disciple of Jesus Christ. You can't be a disciple of Jesus if you're a puppet! If you're only 10 percent alive, you can only be a 10-percent disciple.

Experience reality; come to your senses. That will bring you to the now. That will bring you to experience. It is in the now that God is found.

But is that prayer? Prayer is speaking with God, isn't it? That's right, praying is speaking with God.

But think about a mother who is ill, and her daughter cleans the whole house, prepares food, takes care of the yard. She isn't talking to her mother, but how much she is telling her!

Enter into life and you will be serving the cause of Jesus Christ…who calls us not simply to a new religion, but to life.

Six

Freedom

A Japanese general was arrested by his enemies and thrown in prison. The man knew that the next day he was going to be tortured. He couldn't sleep; he kept pacing his cell, thinking about death. But suddenly he reached a conclusion: "When is it that I am going to be tortured? Tomorrow. But tomorrow isn't real. That's what the Zen masters have taught me!" As soon as he understood that he calmed down and went to sleep. By understanding that the only thing real is the now, he fell asleep. He was in prison, but he was a free man. The enemies of freedom aren't outside; they're inside. The chains that tie us down are here. I want to speak about these chains one by one, because there are many of them.

The first chain that ties us down and keeps us from being free is past experiences. That is quite easy to understand. Someone who has lost his or her mother at eight years of age has been traumatized by this experience and is prevented from getting close to anyone else. A woman who has been sexually molested as a child is afraid of all men. A man unjustly accused and fired from his job finds his entire life poisoned by bitterness.

How are we to break these chains, how be free again? There is a very simple exercise that can help us. Performing it profitably requires faith and gratitude.

If you discover that you are being influenced by one of these bad experiences from the past, go back to this experience in a moment of peace, calm, and serenity. If you don't succeed, talk to God and keep calm. Imagine you are alongside God, telling him, "Lord, it's hard but I believe and trust that if you have allowed this to happen it has been for my good. I may not even see where the good is, but I know that it exists for me." Do this gently. Don't be violent; don't force yourself. If you find that you are too disturbed, drop it, and continue another day. But it is important, once the exercise has begun, to take it to the end. You may feel anger taking over your heart. That's okay, be angry. Even so, you will be praying. The Lord will be happy about your honesty. Then put it aside for another day. It is something that takes time, because freedom is not acquired quickly. When you feel in your heart and tell God that you really believe that everything has served for your good, go on to the next step: thank God. When you can be grateful for the event and for the good that will come from it, you will feel free; the chain will be broken. One thing less to tie you down.

~ Another kind of chain that seizes us within: good experiences from the past. How? It is so good to recall them and be nourished by them. There is danger there, however. The danger is that you get stuck in that illness called nostalgia, that you stop living! You will abandon the present. In fact you will probably destroy the present.

Let us suppose you have had a marvelous experience with a friend, watching the sunset, for example. Another time, you go out for a walk with him. If you are attached to your beautiful past experience of that sunset and enclose it in a silver locket, carrying it around with you while you walk along with your friend, secretly you open your silver locket, take a look, and say, "The present is not as good as the past experience!" See what you are doing? Because of your experience from the past you have destroyed the present. You will be less free, less alive. The experience of the past has you chained!

How can you free yourself of this? There is a method that can be very painful. Giving birth to new life can hurt. But if you are willing, think about some of the people that you have loved in the past and who are no longer with you because of separation or death. Talk to each of these persons, saying, "I have had the good fortune that you have come into my life! How thankful I am to you! I will always love you! Now, goodbye, I have to go. If I attach myself to you I won't learn to love the present, and I won't learn to love the persons I'm with. Goodbye!" This can be painful.

There is another exercise that some of you may find more painful: think about some of your possessions from the past, things that you have treasured, such as your youth, your strength, your beauty. Personalize them. That may sound somewhat childish. But don't be afraid of being like a child. You may find the kingdom! Talk with them and say, "How wonderful it was having you! How grateful I am for having had you in my life! But now, goodbye, I have to go!" Many old people have never lived and have never tested all the sweetness, depth, and riches that old age brings, because they have never left their youth, strength, and vitality behind. The best is still to come. Many people lose out on the best period of their lives, their advancing days, because they are too centered on the past, chained to the good experiences of the past.

Thus we have two chains keeping us from being happy. An injured bird can't fly, but a bird that remains stuck on a tree branch can't either. Stop being stuck in the past! The Hindu proverb goes,

"Water is purified by flowing, the human being by going forward."

~~~ Now comes the third chain: anxiety and fear of the future. Remember the Japanese general about to be tortured? Jesus talks about the same attitude in more poetic language: "Look at the birds of the air, look at the lilies of the field. They're not worried. Therefore, do not be anxious!" How hard it is to attain that reality! Even Jesus despaired in the face of death. He was depressed and anxious. And if we want to break the chain of anxiety, we have to do what Jesus did: face the fear and talk to it as though it were a person. Lovingly, without violence, because the fear is inside us, disguised as caution. Say to the fear, "I understand why you are here, but I trust in God." And if you find in your heart that you can do it, be grateful in advance for these consequences. That will be a great help. Thank God for everything that is going to happen.

The next internal chain that enslaves us also has to do with the future: ambition. Being ambitious can be a wonderful thing. But being enslaved by ambition is horrible. People ruled by ambition don't even live! There's no need to explain this. We all know people like that. What are you to do if you are a victim of ambition? Put yourself in the presence of God, make an act of faith that the future is in God's hands. Say to God, "Lord, I trust that you have control over the future. I am going to do everything I can to achieve my dreams, but I leave the result in your hands." Afterward be thankful for what results from such an attitude. This will bring you peace and freedom.

The next chain is attachment to present things. The human heart is a big magnet, and I don't have to tell you that, because every human being experiences it. We want to possess things and persons and let nothing separate us from them. We are dependent, and we lose our freedom. Often we don't let people be free either. I suggest an exercise to free our hearts from this type of attachment. Think about a person to whom you are deeply attached, so attached that you don't want to leave him or her. Talk to this person in your thinking, imagine this person seated in front of you, and speak to him or her. Talk in a friendly way. Tell this person what he or she means to you and then add the following formula, which you will find painful at first. But as I said from the beginning, don't force yourselves. If it is painful, leave it for later, when you are able. Tell the person, "How precious you are to me, how much I love you, but you are not my life! I have a life to live, a destiny to fulfill that is different from yours." These are hard words, but life isn't always easy.

Then take things, places, occupations, valuable things from which it is hard to separate yourself, and say something similar to each of them, "How precious you are to me! But you are not my life. I have a life to live, a destiny to fulfill that is different from yours." Afterward say the same thing to realities more intimately connected to you, things that are almost part of your being: reputation, health. Tell life itself that someday it will be annihilated by death: "How you are precious and loved, but you are not my life. I have a life to live and a destiny to fulfill, different from you." By courageously repeating that phrase, you can hope to attain spiritual freedom.

~~~ There is another chain to which I have to alert you. We have spoken about unpleasant experiences from the past, good experiences from the past, fear of the future, future ambitions, and attachment to the present. And now comes what I regard as the most powerful chain of all, the hardest one to break.

But let's do an exercise. You may not be able to do it; you may need a little more time and peace to manage to do it. The exercise consists of asking, "What existed a hundred years earlier here where I am sitting?" Use your imagination. Then a bigger jump: "What existed three thousand years ago where I am sitting?"—a thousand years, that is, before the birth of Jesus Christ. Even that is still relatively recent, since scientists tell us that life has existed on our planet for millions of years. "And three thousand years from now, what will exist on this point where I am sitting? Will there be a desert here? Will there be a forest? Will there be another civilization?" Of one thing you can be certain: if there are people there, they won't be speaking your language; they won't be wearing your clothes; they will belong to another culture. No language has survived as a living language for three thousand years. Try to imagine this, as though you were looking at the earth three thousand years from now, looking for this place, seeking some remnant of your life.

You will experience a feeling of immensity, a feeling of liberation. From the illusion that you are important. Except in God's eyes, we are not so important. Think about those sparrows that Jesus talks about, think about the lilies, about all the flowers in the field. Think about the grains of sand, drops of water, a raindrop. Think about yourselves. How insignificant we are!

If you are able to perform this exercise successfully, you will be free of the greatest tyranny of all, the tyranny of the self. You will experience liberation, relief, and freedom because there is no one so free and so alive as the person who has accepted death and his or her own insignificance. This exercise will give you perspective and a sense of vastness. But you need time.

I have still another exercise to recommend, a "mysterious exercise" because it does not immediately make plain the connection between this exercise and freedom. It consists of the following: get in contact with your bodily sensations; and after having done that for a few moments, become aware that you are observing these sensations. And say, "I am not these sensations, I am not this body." Then observe the thoughts that are in your mind. After some time turn your attention to the one observing the thoughts and say, "I am not these thoughts; I am not my thoughts." Then stay alert to your feelings or remember some past feelings, especially from the recent past — anxieties, depressions, blame, whatever. After some time, turn your attention to the one observing these feelings or toward the one remembering the feelings and say, "I am not this feeling, I am not my feelings."

If you are anxious, don't identify with your anxiety. If you are depressed, don't identify with that depression. "I am not that depression."

This is one of the great exercises given in the East. Its results are not immediately noticeable. But it works without fail. And it breaks the most deep-seated of chains, that of the illusion and tyranny of the self.

Remain in silence for a few minutes and practice some of the exercises that I have suggested and that you have found attractive.

~~~ Let me tell you a story about a free person. It is the story of a girl in a fishing village who became a single mother. Her parents beat her until she stated who the father was: "It was the Zen master who lives in the temple outside the village." Her parents and all the villagers were outraged. They hurried to the temple after the baby was born and left it in front of the Zen master. And they said, "You hypocrite, this child is yours! Take care of it!" All the master said was, "Very well! Very well!" And he gave the baby to one of the women in the

village to care for, and the master provided for the expenses. After this the master lost his reputation, his disciples left him, no one went to consult him, and this went on for some months. When the girl saw this, she couldn't hold back anymore and she finally revealed the truth. The child's father wasn't the master but a neighbor boy. When her parents and the whole village had learned this, they returned to the temple and bowed down before the master. They begged him for forgiveness, and asked him to return the child to them. The master returned the baby, and all he said was, "Very well! Very well!" That is a free person—a person able to suffer, who has attained the perspective I was telling you about. My desire for me and for you is that, as a result of our feeble efforts, God may give us that gift!

Seven

Love

So far I've spoken to you about peace, happiness, silence, life, and freedom. I now want to speak about love. This is the most difficult topic because love is something so vast that it is almost like God himself, in its immensity and mystery. We occasionally get a glimpse of love and we vaguely understand it. But I don't think anyone really understands this mysterious reality. I am going to consider two aspects of love: love as creation and love as identification.

~~~ I begin speaking about love as creation by telling you a wonderful story from the American Indians, one of my favorites.

Once long ago an Indian warrior found an eagle's egg on a mountaintop, and he put this eagle's egg next to the eggs that a hen was going to be sitting on. When the time came, the chicks hatched, and so did the little eagle, who had been kept warmed in the same brood. The tiny eagle grew alongside the hatchlings. After some time it learned to cackle like chickens, to scratch the ground, to look for worms, and it limited itself to going up into the lower branches of the bushes just like all the other chickens. And it kept living with the idea that it was a chicken. One day when it was old, the eagle was looking up to the sky and saw something magnificent. Up there in the bright blue, a majestic bird was flying in the open sky, with seeming effortlessness. The old eagle was awestruck. It turned to the nearest chicken and said, "What kind of a bird is that?" The chicken looked up and answered, "Oh, that's the golden eagle, the queen of the skies. But don't pay any attention to it. You and I are here down below." The eagle never again looked up, and it died thinking it was a chicken. That was how everyone treated it, and that was how it grew up, lived, and died.

~~~ Love as creation means looking at the eagle in ourselves, being aware of who we really are in order to be able to open our wings and soar. And so we create the eagle in ourselves.

A famous American psychologist oversaw a remarkable experiment. He and his team gave all the students in a school an IQ test shortly before the end of the school year. They then chose ten students and told each of their teachers, "These ten children are going to be in your class. We know from their tests that technically they are what we call mentally gifted. You are going to see that all of them are going to be at the top of the class the next school year. You only have to promise never to tell that to the class because it might be harmful to them." And so the teachers promised not to say anything. The fact is that none of those on the list was mentally gifted and the experiment simply amounted to choosing ten names at random and giving them to the teachers. A year later the psychologists returned to the school. They tested all the children. All the "mentally gifted" had increased their IQ by at least ten points. Some rose thirty-six points. The psychologists interviewed the teachers and asked, "What did you think of these children?" The teachers quickly used adjectives like "intelligent," "dynamic," "lively," "interested," and so forth.

What might have happened with these children if their teachers had not thought of them as mentally gifted in the classroom? It was the teachers who developed all the potential of these students.

The psychologists repeated the experiment several times in other schools, and even with animals, always successfully. They told psychology students who were carrying out experiments with rats, "We are going to give you a new breed of rat that will perform better." And the rats performed better, even though they were the same breed as the others. They came to the conclusion that it was because the students paid more attention to them. They expected more of the rats, and the rats met their expectations, which were somehow communicated to the animals.

The first time I heard about this experiment, I was reminded of a great American, Father Flanagan, the founder of Boys Town. This man became a legend, and his fame even reached India. Initially, he set up his home to help abandoned children, and later to help delinquents. When the police no longer knew what to do, Father Flanagan took them home with him. As the story goes, he never failed with his boys. I remember one story along these lines that left a very vivid impression on me.

An eight-year-old boy killed his father and mother. Can you imagine what must have happened to this child that he should become so violent at such a young age? He was arrested a number of times for bank robbery. The police didn't know what to do with him: he was a child so they couldn't arrest him or put him on trial or send him to a reform school because he had to be at least twelve years old for that. They called Father Flanagan and said, "Will you accept this kid?" The priest answered, "Of course, send him over!"

Many years later, the boy wrote his own story. "I remember the day when I was on my way to Boys Town in a train, with a police officer, and I was thinking, 'They're sending me to a priest. If this man says he loves me, I'm going to kill him.' " And the boy was a killer!

He went to Boys Town and the story continues: he knocked on the door and Father Flanagan said, "Come in!" The boy went in and Father Flanagan said, "What's your name?"

And the boy said, "Dave, sir."

And Father Flanagan said, "Dave! Welcome to Boys Town. We've been expecting you! Now that you're here, you must want to take a walk to become familiar with everything. You know that everyone works for a living here? Someone will show you everything. Perhaps you can choose an occupation, but for now take it easy, take a look around at the place. You can go now. I'll see you later."

And the boy said that these few seconds changed his life. "For the first time in my life, I looked in the eyes of a man who, without using words, said not that he loved me, but 'You're good, you're not bad, you're good!' " The boy became good. As psychologists tell us, we tend to be what we feel we are. Can you think of anything more spiritual and divine than that? That we should see the goodness in someone, that we should communicate that to the person, who thereby is changed. The person is re-created. "The lover creates love," that is, sees the beauty there, and by seeing it, draws it out.

People often used to ask Father Flanagan the reason for his success. Father Flanagan didn't answer the question, because the principle that he followed was, "There's no such thing as a bad boy." Flanagan saw the goodness and made that goodness spring out of each boy that he took in. He created goodness.

That is what I want to communicate to you as love. Would you like to have a bit of Father Flanagan's perception? I'm sure we would all like to be like him, because we all want to love.

If we want to develop that kind of perception, we have to enter into a school of love. We have to do exercises that aren't extremely difficult, but they're not too easy either.

Begin with the following: think about someone that you love deeply. Imagine that this person is seated in front of you; speak with that person lovingly. Tell this person what he or she means to you, what their coming into your life has meant. And as you do that, be aware of what you feel. When you have warmed up, move to the next exercise.

Think about someone you don't like. You are standing in front of this person. As you look at him or her, try to see some good there. Make an effort to see the good. If you find it hard to do that, you can imagine that Jesus is standing next to you and that he is looking at that person. He will be your teacher in the art of looking and in the art of loving. What is there to be seen? What goodness, what beauty can be detected in the person? If Jesus were to return to earth, what do you think would be the first thing he would observe in humankind? The immense goodness, confidence, and sincerity of pure love. There are oceans of goodness within human beings. He would spot that immediately because the good person sees goodness everywhere. Evil people see evil because they tend to see themselves in others, seeing others as a reflection of themselves. Imagine Jesus looking at you. What will he see?

We go on to the third, and probably the hardest, exercise. But if you really want to love, you have to go through it. Imagine Jesus right there in front of you. He talks with you about all the goodness and beauty and all the qualities that he sees in you. If you are like most people, you are probably going to begin to accuse yourself of all kinds of defects and sins, and Jesus is going to accept that. When he saw evil, he called it by its name and condemned it. But he never condemned the sinner, even while condemning the sin.

Think about how he looked at a prostitute in the gospel story. And how he looked at a thief, at a hardened publican, and even at the Pharisees and at the persons who were crucifying him. There he is right in front of you! And you are accusing yourself of all your sins, and he is accepting them, admitting that you have all these defects. But he understands, makes concessions. These defects do not interfere with the goodness and beauty that he sees in you. That isn't hard to understand. Think about yourself. Think about someone you love. If you really look at the other person, that person has defects. And even these defects do not constrain your love, nor keep you from seeing the goodness in that person. Imagine Jesus doing that. And see the effect that it has on you. Accept the love of Jesus and of those who love you.

The gospels tell us that when Jesus met Simon Peter for the first time, the Master saw in this man what no one could suspect was there, and he called him rock, stone. And that was what brought about change in Peter. Imagine, then, that Jesus is standing there before you. What name would he give you?

〜〜Before going on to another aspect of love, I want to tell you a Western fairy tale. You're aware that fairy tales contain a great deal of wisdom. This is the story of the frog and the princess.

One day the beautiful princess went walking through the forest and found a frog. The frog greeted her very courteously. The princess was startled at a frog speaking human language. But the frog said to her, "Your royal highness, I'm not really a frog. I'm a prince, but a witch turned me into a frog."

The princess, who was a kindhearted person, replied, "Is there something I can do to break this spell?"

The frog replied, "Yes, the witch said that if I found a princess that I loved who stayed with me three days and three nights, the spell would be broken and I would be a prince again."

The princess could already see the prince in that frog. She took the frog with her to the palace. Everyone said, "What a repugnant creature, and she is carrying it around!"

And she replied, "No, it's not a repugnant creature, it's a prince!" And she kept the prince with her night and day, on the table, and placed him on the pillows beside her while she slept. After three days and three nights, she woke up and saw that young and handsome prince, who kissed her hand with gratitude because she had broken the spell and changed him back into the prince that he was. This fairy tale is the story of all of us. Somehow we have been changed into frogs, and we go through life looking for someone who will break the spell and re-create us! Is your Jesus like that? Is your God like that? Do we meet many people like Father Flanagan?

God is unknown. But when we make an image of God, is God at least as good as the best of us? Does your God perhaps say, "Angels! Trumpets! Here comes the prince! Here comes the princess!" Is that how God treats you? Even seeing all our faults? We should think about this, because we tend to transform ourselves into the God we adore.

〜〜 Now let us consider love as identification. In India mystics and poets have often asked themselves who the holy person is. And they have come up with beautiful answers.

"The holy person is like a rose." Have you ever heard a rose say, "I am going to give my fragrance only to good people who smell me, and I am going to deny my perfume to evil people"? No, it is of the very nature of the rose to spread fragrance.

"The holy person is like a lamp lit in a dark room." Can a lamp say that it is going to shed light only on good people and keep from shining on bad people?

"The holy person is like a tree giving shade to both good and bad people. The tree gives its shade even to the person cutting it down. And if it is aromatic, it will leave its smell after being cut."

Isn't this just what Jesus says when he tells us to be merciful like our heavenly Father who makes it rain on the good and the evil? Who makes the sun shine on the just and sinners? How will we one day be able to reach that kind of love? Through understanding, through an understanding, or mystical experience. Have you yet experienced that millions of us make up a single Christ? Paul says that we are all a single body, members of one another. This is the image of the body. Just like my body and me. There aren't two of us, but we aren't the same thing. I am not my body, but there aren't two of us! And how I love my body! When a part of my body is ill or healthy, I love it just the same. So this is the understanding that is given to some fortunate people. They are different from others, but they are not separate—they are one body.

There is a Hindu story about seven crazy men who go to a village for a kind of huge banquet and go back home late at night, drunk and crazier than before. It begins to rain, and they take shelter under a tree. When they wake up the next morning they begin to moan loudly. A passerby stops and says, "What is going on?"

"We slept under this tree and our hands and legs are all mixed up. So we don't know whose hands and legs belong to whom."

And the passerby says, "That's easy, give me a thorn!" He then pokes a leg and its owner yells, "Ow!" The passerby says, "This is your leg!" He keeps poking different hands and legs and separating the crazy men.

When someone is hurt or mistreated and I say, "Ouch!" something has happened: love as identification. Can we do anything to obtain that grace? No, it is a gift. All we can do is prepare ourselves. You may not believe it, but I said that if you were to sit down and look, or if you were to sit down and get in contact with yourself, you would achieve silence and things would be revealed to you. All we do is prepare the soil. And if you practice this exercise that I am recommending, you will be preparing yourself for this grace. Some day, hopefully, it will be given to you.

Dedication to the exercises in this book will bring good results for everyone, but love as identification, only God can give that.

God is the Unknown, God is the Mystery, God is Love. And so whenever you are loving, you are sharing in divinity and grace.

In a world where minds are corrupted and suspicious, can you think of a better route to God?

Eight

Prayer

There are so many things I would like to speak to you about! But there is one matter that people always question me about. When they find out that I am a Catholic priest, they ask me, "Could you help us pray better?"

I've gone on to ask myself: How could we pray better? I think we have to go back to the notion of prayer that we transmit and live, beginning with everything that prayer is not. There's a story that provides a good illustration.

A young man went to a great master of wisdom and said to him, "Master, so great is my trust in God that I didn't even hitch my camel out there. I left it to God's providence, for him to take care of."

And the wise master said, "Go back outside and tie your camel to the post, you nincompoop!

There's no point in inconveniencing God with something that you can do yourself."

Very clear, right? It is important that we have this attitude in mind when we talk about prayer. God doesn't have to be bothered with things that we can do ourselves.

I recall the story of a rabbi who served God faithfully for his whole lifetime. One day he said to God, "Lord, I've been a devoted worshiper and obedient to the law. I have been a good Jew, but now I'm old and I need help: Lord, let me win the lottery so I'll have a peaceful old age!" And he prayed, and prayed, and prayed. A month went by, then two, three, five, a whole year passed, three years went by. One day in desperation the man said, "God, take care of it!"

And God said, "Take care of it yourself! Why don't you buy a ticket?"

〰〰 That gives the idea of what prayer is not. But what is prayer? I want to tell another story.

Prayer

A man invented fire. Having invented it, he headed north where there were tribes in high snowy mountains, and he began to teach them his fire-making skill. He showed them the value of warming themselves in the winter, cooking their food, and using fire in construction. And they learned enthusiastically. As soon as they learned, the inventor of the art went somewhere else without giving them time to thank him, because he was a great man.

Great people do not need to be remembered or shown gratitude. So he vanished and went on to another tribe. And there he began to teach them to make fire. That tribe also became enthusiastic, and he went on becoming more and more famous. Then the priests, fearing that their own popularity would decline, decided to get rid of him, and so they poisoned him. But to prevent the people from becoming suspicious, the priests did this: they put up a picture of the man; they put it on the highest altar in the temple and told the people to venerate the great inventor of fire. They also had all the fire-making tools put on the highest altar for everyone to worship. They developed a ritual and a whole liturgy for venerating the tools and the inventor of the art of making fire. Veneration and adoration were passed on for decades and decades, centuries and centuries, but there was no fire. Where is prayer? In the fire! Where is the fire? In prayer! There it is! What you have done to find the fire is prayer. You pray for weeks, months, and years, and there's no fire. No prayer, no prayer. Lots of good will, but no prayer.

"Why do you call me Lord, Lord, and do not do what I say? And you will come and say: 'Lord we did miracles in your name,' and I will say to you: I do not know you, I am not interested!" He was less interested in the "Lord, Lord" than in us. He was more interested in "why you do not do what I say." But we have to be careful with this. Don't think that your good works are necessarily prayer. "If I hand over my body to be burned and all my goods to feed the poor, and do not have love, it will all be in vain." Some good works are really good, and others are corrupt. Master Eckhart, the great German mystic, says, "You should be less concerned about what you have to do and think more about what you must be. For if your being is good, your work will be of great value." It is being that must be transformed; that's where the fire is!

How are you going to transform your being? What will you do? Nothing! In order to be transformed, you have to see. See something that transforms you. No one is changed by working on himself or herself. You know how to fix lots of things and that's a great gift, but if you try to fix persons you'll run into problems. You don't have to fix anything; you have to see things in a new way. Change comes through seeing. Metanoia, repentance, for the reign of God has arrived! Repentance doesn't mean weeping over sins; repentance means looking at everything in a new way. Change of idea, transformation of the heart. Like the man who said to his wife, "I've changed my mind." And she said, "Thank God, I hope the new one works better!" There you have it! Literally another mind, another way of looking at things. A new way of seeing everything. That is the transformation we're talking about.

When that happens, you will change. Your works will change, and so will your life. That's the fire! How do you need to see things a new way? There's no need for strength, no need to be useful, no need to be self-confident, no strength of will, no effort. What is needed is good will to think about what is not customary, good will to see something new. And that's the last thing that human beings want. People don't want to see anything different from what they've always seen. That's why Jesus had so many problems when he came with his Good News. People don't like to hear about good things. We want to suffer, we want to feel miserable, in order not to know. We unconsciously desire to cause suffering. We don't like the good part of the Good News, and we don't like the new part of the Good News.

Are you ready to see things in another way? Pay attention: don't accept everything I'm saying just because I'm saying it; that won't do you any good. Don't swallow anything from me. I am very fond of Buddha's words, "Monks and disciples ought not to accept my words out of respect." What has to be done is like what the goldsmith does with gold: polishing, scraping, cutting, mixing. That is the way to do things. You have to stay open, receptive, and always ready to question, to think for yourselves. Otherwise you fall into rigidity, into mental laziness. We don't want that.

~~~ Are you suffering? Do you have problems? Do you hate every minute of your life?

Have you enjoyed the past three hours, every second of the past three hours? If the answer is no, if the answer is that you are suffering, disturbed, you really have problems. There is something wrong with you. Seriously wrong. You're asleep, you're dead!

I bet most of you have never heard anyone talk like that. The usual thing is to say that it's natural to have problems, that suffering is natural. In that case, I'd better explain a little about what suffering is. You can be in pain and suffering or you can be in pain and not suffer.

A certain master was asked by his disciple, "What has enlightenment brought you?" And he said, "Before enlightenment, I used to go around depressed; after enlightenment, I remain depressed!" But there is a great difference. Suffering means letting yourself be disturbed by depression. That is suffering. This much should be clear by now. Suffering means letting oneself be disturbed by pain, by depression, by anxiety.

In the process of learning prayer, depression keeps coming and so does anxiety. And they can mean clouds passing in the sky and your being identified with the clouds. But you can be the sky, detached from them. And they keep coming and going: "Before enlightenment, I used to go around depressed; after enlightenment, I remain depressed."

Where do you think suffering comes from? Some say from life. Life is hard, life is difficult! The Chinese have a wonderful notion: "In the whole universe there's nothing as cruel as nature.

There's no escaping from it. But it isn't nature that causes catastrophes. It is the human heart which is the source of feeling." It isn't life that's difficult; we make it that way.

Someone in New York told me that an African tribe had no way to remove from their midst those who had been found guilty. So they banished them, cursed them, exiled them, and in a week the man or woman died. They simply died. We might say, "They killed them! Sentencing them to exile killed them!" No, if you and I were banished, we would suffer a little, but we wouldn't die. So did they kill themselves? The way they experienced exile is what killed them.

You've heard about students who take their exams so seriously that if they fail they commit suicide? If you and I were to flunk we wouldn't kill ourselves. So what do you think killed such students? Failing? No. How they reacted to failing.

When you plan a picnic and it rains, what causes you to feel bad? The rain? Or your reaction? Awareness of this shocks people who have prayed for decades but have never become aware of this fact. It is one of the risks of prayer: it can prevent you from getting to the fire.

Now think about something that is bothering you. Or about something that has bothered you in the recent past. And try to understand that the disturbance does not come from outside, from the event, from things, from the fact that someone has died, that you have made a mistake, that you have come across an accident, lost your job or money. None of that comes from outside. It comes from how you react to the event, the person, the thing that disturbs you. If someone else were in your place, it is possible that he or she would not be disturbed. You are.

Once in St. Louis a priest came to me and said he had a friend with AIDS. And he said something strange was happening to his friend, who said, "I began to live only when the doctor said I had AIDS and that death was certain." Do you believe that? The priest said to me, "I've known more or less thirty people in this same situation and twelve or fifteen have told me something similar."

Why do people react so differently to the same stimulus? This is a matter of their programming. Did someone fail to fulfill a promise to you, has someone rejected you, has someone left you? No, no one has hurt you in your whole life! Nothing that has happened has ever disturbed you. It was you who did it to yourself. Actually this wasn't even done by you, because no one would do it deliberately. Your conditioning, your programming, has caused everything: how you see things and life. That is what has to be changed: your "head"!

~~~ Let's go on to another test. Think about some problem with someone, with anyone. You may think that that person is untrustworthy, annoying, lazy, temperamental, and deserves to be rejected.

If you have problems with people get ready for a shock: there's something wrong with you. There are no problems in dealing with human beings. If you change, everything will change. If you can bring yourself to let go, people will change. You aren't seeing people as they are but as you are. If someone causes me to be bothered, and in a bad mood, there's something wrong with me. I have to change! How can I give someone the power to upset me? How give someone the power to decide whether I'm going to be happy or sad? If I give that power to someone, I can't protect myself from the consequences of what I'm doing. "In nature there are neither rewards nor punishments, only consequences." You only have to grow and face them.

We have to have the courage to not let ourselves be manipulated. We are afraid to say no, we're afraid to tell others to take care of their own lives. "Live your life. Let me live mine!"

If we don't do this, there's no way of avoiding the consequences of letting ourselves be manipulated.

Our happiness is never caused by some thing. True happiness is uncaused. If a person is causing you happiness, or if your job is causing you happiness, it's actually not happiness. It's having a desire satisfied: I want something, I get it, I'm excited, I feel gratified, I feel pleasure, and I'm tired of it after a while. If I don't get it, I'm anxious. That's not happiness! It's emotion. Satisfying a desire.

Sometimes I think that almost everyone has been programmed to be unhappy. We can't not be unhappy. And we go through life with ups and downs, or back and forth, suffering. I repeat: happiness is uncaused. When nothing can hurt you, no person, no event, nothing, then you will be happy. What do you do to be happy? Nothing! You don't do anything. You have to be detached from things. From illusion. From mistaken ideas. How are you to be detached? By seeing that they are wrong.

Remember the African tribe I was talking about? Why did the exiles die? Because they had been banished? No, because they added something to their situation, something to their program. Your unhappiness is caused by something that you have added. This addition is the cause of unhappiness. How do you become healed? Get rid of your illness and be healthy! Health isn't a thing; it's the absence of disease.

When the eye is unobstructed, the result is seeing; when the ear is unobstructed, the result is hearing; when the palate is unobstructed, the result is tasting. When the mind is unobstructed, the result is wisdom and happiness. If you could get rid of illusion, you would be happy.

I have seen persons with very poor health, with cancer, experiencing intense pain, and yet happy! They aren't suffering because suffering means struggling. Suffering means asking, "How much longer is this going to last?" The present moment is never intolerable.What is intolerable is what is going to happen in the next four hours. Having your body here at eight at night, and your mind at ten thirty, that's what causes problems. Having your body in São Paulo and your mind in Manaus, that's what causes suffering.

~~~ So go tie up your camel, you nincompoop. God can't be inconvenienced with things that we can do ourselves.

Prayer and fire! Fire meaning transformation that comes through seeing one's illusion and becoming detached from it.

You are seated in a theater listening to a concert. Suddenly you remember that you forgot to lock your car. You're anxious. You can't get up and lock your car, you can't concentrate on the symphony, you're caught between both of them. What a fascinating image of life!

Let me complete this image with a Japanese story of a boy who was running away from a tiger. He came to a cliff, and began to slip down, but caught onto a branch of a tree that was growing on the edge of the cliff. He looked up and saw the tiger looking at him, and there was no way of going back up. He looked down and saw the bottom of a canyon six thousand feet below, and alongside him a tree with fruit. The fruit was ripe. So he picked a piece of fruit, raised it to his mouth, and experienced how sweet it was! There he learned to live life one moment at a time, the only way to live. But this sounds like an impossible order.

Have you heard how the South African mines were discovered? There was a traveler seated at the door of the village chief's house. He saw the chief's children playing with things that looked like marbles. He picked one of them up and his heart exploded with joy. It was a diamond! So he went to tell the village chief: "My children also play with these stones; they call them marbles. Could I take some of them home with me? I'd be happy to give you tobacco in exchange."

The chief answered, "We have millions of them here. It would be robbery to accept your tobacco, but I'll accept whatever you give me." The man gave him the tobacco, went home, sold the diamonds, came back, bought all that land, and became the richest man in the world. Here's the point of this story: those people were walking on top of a treasure and didn't know it. Life is a banquet and yet most people are depriving themselves of it. They never discover the treasure.

If prayer were suitably practiced and understood, it would provide the wealth that would make things unimportant. "Life is something that happens when we're busy with something else." We're busy trying to impress everyone. We're busy trying to win the Olympics. We're busy being successful. And life passes us by.

~~~ There's something else inside us that is precious. A precious pearl. A treasure. The reign of God is inside us. If we would only discover that! The great tragedy of life lies not in how much we suffer but in how much we miss. Human beings are born asleep, live asleep, and die asleep. Maybe we're not born asleep; we're born awake, but as the brain develops, we fall asleep. We have children asleep, raise children asleep, handle big business deals asleep, enter government office asleep, and die asleep. We never wake up. This is what spirituality is about: waking up. We're living in a drunken stupor. It's as though we were hypnotized, drugged! And we don't know what we're missing.

How to get out of this? How to wake up? How are we going to know we're asleep?

The mystics, when they see what surrounds them, discover an extra joy flowing in the heart of things. With one voice they speak about this joy and love flowing everywhere. And even if they have pain, or what we call suffering, there is a tremendous joy that nothing can change or take away from them. How attain that? Through understanding. By being liberated from illusions and wrong ideas. We have to get rid of them, because it is useless to keep saying to God, "Give me! Give me! Give me!" Go tie up your camel! God can't be bothered with things that we can do ourselves.

They told a man whose beard was on fire, "Your beard is in flames!" And he said, "Can't you see I'm praying for rain! I'm doing something!" We say, "Lord that I may see!" and remain with our eyes closed. Understanding, attention, willingness to see: that is prayer.

There are two kinds of prayer. There's the "Lord, Lord," and something much better, "Do what I say." There are people who do what he says, without ever saying, "Lord, Lord," and even without ever having heard talk about the Lord. There are people who are full of "Lord, Lord," who pray day and night, but risk being told, "I don't know you." "Do what I say": that is love of God. Being transformed in love: that is love of God. Then you will know who God is. Then you will know what reality is.

Nine

Liberation

Think about a little child on whom a drug has been tried. When it grows up its whole body cries out for the drug. Living without it is a pain so great that it is better to die. You and I, like that child, have taken this drug that is called "approval," "appreciation," "success," "acceptance," "popularity." Once you have taken the drug, society can control you; you've become a robot.

How do human beings become robots? Listen to this: "Oh, you're so pretty." And the robot swells with pride. I push the appreciation button and it's riding high. Then I push the other button, the criticism one, and it hits bottom. Complete control. We are so affected by approval! So easily controllable. And when deprived of it, we are frightened, afraid of making mistakes, afraid that people are going to laugh.

I saw a three-year-old girl go into a dining room all dressed up. We all clapped, but she thought we were laughing at her and went running away at top speed. Her mother had to go find her, but she didn't want to come back. She thought we had laughed at her. She was only three and we'd already made a little monkey out of her. Someone taught her that. When you do such and such people will applaud, and she should feel good. And when we go "Booo!" she has to feel bad. Once you've taken this drug, it's all over.

Do you think Jesus Christ was controlled by what people thought of him or said about him? People who are awake don't need that drug.

When you make a mistake and are rejected you feel a tremendous vacuum. Your loneliness is such that you go back to being pulled along begging for that drug called encouragement and acceptance, and you continue to be controlled. How are we to get out of this? Because you've taken this drug, you've lost your ability to love. You can no longer see any human being. You're only aware of whether people accept you or don't, approve of you or don't. You see them as threatening your drug or helping you get it.

Think about politicians. Often politicians don't see people at all. They see votes, and if you're not a help or a threat to their getting votes, they won't even notice you.

Business people see only money. They don't see people, only business deals.

When under the effect of this drug we're no different. How can we love what we don't even see? How can we become free of the drug? We have to pull these tentacles out of our system. They've gotten down into our bones. Such is the control that society exerts over us. If we can do that, everything will be the same, but we will have become detached. We will be in the world, but we will not be of the world. That is terrifying. It is like asking an addict, "Why don't you enjoy a good and nutritious meal, fresh water from a mountain spring, and the pleasant morning air? Put aside your drug for this!" He can't even conceive of such an idea, because he can't live without the drug.

How to get out of this? The fear has to be faced. We have to understand why we can't live without people's approval. How to love people? Die to them. Die to the need for people. Understand what the drug is doing to you.

Be patient with yourself. Then call the drug by its name: it is an artificial stimulant. Do you really want to live? Savor your senses, your mind. Appreciate your work, nature, go to the mountains and appreciate the trees and the stars, the night. Send the crowds away. And you will be completely alone. Then love will be born in solitude. You reach the country of love by passing through the country of death. And you will realize that your heart has taken you to a vast desert. At first you will feel lonely. You aren't used to enjoying persons without depending on them.

At the end of the process, you will be able to see them. Then you will see that the desert is suddenly transformed into love. And music will play in your heart. It will be spring forever. Provide yourself with adequate nourishment. Call the drug by its name and be patient, just as you would be with an addict.

Think about someone whose approval you think you need, whose appreciation you want. See if you can realize how, vis-à-vis this person, you have lost your freedom. Think about someone whom you need in order to soften the pain of your loneliness. Think of how, with regard to this person, you have lost your freedom. You aren't free! You don't dare to be yourself!

You don't have to impress anyone, ever again. You are completely comfortable with everyone; you no longer desire anything from anyone. Nonfulfillment of your desires does not make you unhappy.

When you no longer have to defend yourself from anyone, you no longer feel the need to make excuses. Or to explain yourself. You don't have to impress anyone. You don't have to be disturbed over what they say or what they think. You don't feel bad. You don't let yourself be affected. That's when love will begin. But only after that.

Liberation

To the extent I need you I can't love you.

"What merit will you have if you greet only those who greet you? And if you love only those who love you? You must be total love like your heavenly Father is all love. For he makes the sun shine on good and evil, and the just and sinners alike."

Ten

Spirituality

Spirituality is being awake. Getting rid of illusions. Spirituality is never being at the mercy of any event, thing, or person. Spirituality means having found the diamond mine inside yourself. Religion is intended to lead you there.

"What good does it do to win the world and lose your soul?" Think about what you feel when you look at a sunset or are in contact with nature. And compare that with your feeling when you are appreciated, applauded, praised. The first kind of feelings, I call feelings of the soul; the second is what I call feelings of the world. Think about the feeling you have when you win a race or an argument, when you get to the top, when you reach success. Feelings of the world. In contrast are your feelings when you are doing some work that you love, when you are immersed in a hobby, reading a book, seeing a film. Feelings of the soul. Think about the times when you have power, when you are the boss, when everyone is looking, and you are on top. What kind of feeling does that create? A worldly feeling! Contrast that feeling with the joy of intimacy, with the company of friends. You appreciate them without being captive to them, laughing and joking. Feelings of the heart.

The feelings of the world aren't natural; they were invented by your society and mine to control us. They don't lead to happiness, only to excitement, emptiness, and anxiety. Think about your own life. Is there even a single day when you aren't consciously or unconsciously oriented toward what others think, feel, or say about you? Your steps are controlled; you march to the drumbeat. Look around. See if you find anyone who is free of such feelings. Feelings of the world! Everywhere you find people chained to feelings of the world, living empty. They have gained the world but lost their souls.

A group of tourists is traveling through a beautiful countryside. But the curtains on the train are drawn and they don't see anything. They are all occupied in deciding who will have the seat of honor, who will be appreciated, who is best, who is prettiest or most talented. This continues to the end of the journey. If you can understand this, you will be free, you will understand what spirituality is.

Then you will discover what reality is, who God is, for you will see yourself detached from one of the greatest illusions: the illusion that we have to be appreciated, beloved, successful, that we must have prestige, honor, power, and popularity. There is only one necessity! That necessity is loving. When you discover that, you are transformed. When life becomes prayer, spirituality overflows into what we do.

Eleven

Clarity

One day I was traveling from the United States to Canada. When we passed the border, the driver said, "We're at the United States border!" We looked down, and, it's funny, you don't see anything. Do you realize that borders exist only in the mind, that in nature there are no border lines? That being an American is just in your mind? That there are no American trees or mountains? Those are conventions! But people are ready to die for those conventions, so real does the separation seem to them.

Have you noticed that Christmas Day exists only in your head? In nature there's no Christmas Day. But look at people seized by Christmas feelings. And there's no New Year's Day. Nor are there illegitimate children. In nature there are no illegitimate children. Illegitimacy is a human convention. Adoption, too, is all in the mind! There are cultures where almost everyone is adopted, and no one is bothered. We react to words, to ideas. We live off ideas, feeding ourselves words.

I recall a farmer whose large property was on the Russian-Finnish border. He had to decide whether he wanted his farm to be in Finland or Russia. He chose Finland. The Russian officials set out to inquire why he didn't want to remain in Russia. He said, "Look, all my life I've wanted to live in our Mother Russia, but now at my age, frankly, I don't think I could endure another Russian winter!"

Love isn't attraction. "I love you more than I love anyone." Translation: I'm more attracted to you than to others. How's that? You attract me more than others. You fit better into my mind's program than other people. That's not very flattering for you, but if my program were different… I'm reminded of people who say, "What does he find in her? Or what does he see in her?" Attraction is blind!

Clarity

An older couple was celebrating sixty years of marriage. They were tired after all the celebration, and as they sat on the porch, the grandfather's feelings were stirred. He said, "Grandma, I admire you!"

"What did you say, Grandfather? Better speak louder. I can't hear without my hearing aid!"

And he said, "I admire you!"

And she said, "I'm tired of you too!"

That's where attraction ends up. Do you feel attracted by someone or something? When you give in to the attraction, gratification follows. And after gratification, weariness or anxiety: "I hope I can keep this up! I hope someone else doesn't move in!" Feelings of possession, jealousy, fear of loss. That's not love!

Love isn't dependence. It is very good to depend on people. If we didn't depend on one another, we wouldn't have society. Interdependence! We depend on the butcher, the baker, the candlestick maker, the pilot, the taxi driver, all kinds of people. But depending on one another in order to be happy, that's what's bad.

Sometimes we see two empty people depending on one another, two incomplete persons propping each other up. Two dominos—one moves and the other falls down. Is that love? Love isn't easing our loneliness! People feel empty inside and rush to fill the emptiness with someone. That isn't love. In order to flee from emptiness and loneliness, people surrender to all kinds of activities, to work, or to someone's arms. But the cure for loneliness isn't contact with human beings; it's contact with reality.

In facing loneliness, we discover that it's not there. There isn't any vacuum! Here's something to remember in the future. What we are looking for is inside us. When we face what's inside us, what we are fleeing disappears. And what we are seeking comes to the surface. Love isn't easing our loneliness. When people talk about love, they're usually talking about a good to be bargained over. "You're good to me? I'll be good to you! You're pleasant to me? I'll be pleasant to you! You're not kind to me? Funny, the pleasant feelings I had about you have turned bitter!" Is that love? That's the market for emotions disguised as attitudes of love.

Love isn't desire. Centuries ago Buddha said, "The world is full of suffering. The origin of suffering, the root of suffering, is desire. Eliminating suffering consists of eliminating desire." By desire he meant that on whose satisfaction my happiness depends. And our society and culture are continually urging us to increase that desire. We are ever more programmed for unhappiness and lovelessness. The world is full of suffering. The root of suffering is desire. Eliminating suffering goes by way of eliminating desire.

Ambition is a brainwashing that has been done on us! We've been told that unless we have ambition, we won't do anything. The energy and delight in work have been forgotten. When an archer shoots for no particular reason, he applies all his skill. When he shoots to win the gold, he becomes blind, loses his reason, sees two targets. It's not his ability that has changed, but the prize.

He is more concerned about winning than about shooting. And the need to win has hollowed out his power. Ambition has taken away his power.

The world is full of suffering, and the root of suffering is desire. Marriages built on desire are fragile, ready to come apart. "I have many expectations of you; you'd better not disappoint me." "You have expectations of me; I'd better fulfill them." Arguments! "You need me! I need you! I need to find my happiness in you! You need to find your happiness in me!" And so the fight begins. That's where the feeling of possession begins. Where that kind of desire exists, there's a threat. And where there's a threat, there's fear. And where there's fear, there's no love. For we always hate what we fear. And perfect love casts out fear! Wherever this kind of desire exists, it always comes accompanied by fear.

Love isn't desire; it's not fixation. Being impassioned is the exact opposite of love, but passion is canonized everywhere. It is an illness that everyone is trying to pass on to us. It can be heard in movies and in love songs. I saw a film where the girl says to the boy, "I love you, I can't live without you!" I can't live without you? Love? That's hunger! When I become impassioned over you, I stop seeing you! Wherever there's a powerful emotion, whether positive or negative, I can't see. Emotion gets in the way and makes me project my own needs on the other.

~~~ We've been speaking thus far about what love is not, and we've come to the end of what can be said about what love is not. It can't be said. When you get rid of your fears, attachments, and illusions, you will know. We walk among illusions.

Love means, at the very least, clarity of perception and precision of response. Seeing the other clearly as he or she is. That is the least that I can ask of love. How can I love you if I don't see you? Usually when we look we don't see one another. We are looking for an image. Does a husband relate to his wife or to an image he has built of her? Does a wife relate to her husband or to an image she has formed of him?

I have an experience of you. This experience is saved in my memory. I make my judgment based on the experience. I carry it with me. I act or react on that basis, not on the basis of what you are now. I look at you through a picture.

When you look at me after a fight and say, "I'm very sorry about that argument," it would be wonderful if I no longer remembered anything. This is what the mystics are talking about when they speak of "purification of the memory." They are not saying forget everything, but empty out the emotion. Be healed of your pain!

You say, "Remember how much in love we were two years ago?" Do you want me to react to that or to you as you are now? When people think of love as investment, they have no idea what love is.

Love is like listening to a symphony, being sensitive to everything in that symphony. It means having a heart sensitive to everyone and to all. Can you imagine that a person would hear a symphony and listen only to the drums? Or value the drums so much that the other instruments would be almost eclipsed? Good musicians, those who love music, listen to each of the instruments; they might have their favorite instruments, but they listen to all of them.

When we are impassioned, when we have a feeling of attachment, an obsession, the object of our passion stands out and other persons are eclipsed.

Love is not a relationship. It is a state of being. Love existed before any human being. Before we existed, love already existed. I've said that when the eye is unobstructed the result is vision. We cannot do anything to get love. If we comprehended our duties, attachments, attractions, obsessions, predilections, inclinations, and if we got rid of them all, love would appear. When the eye is unobstructed, the result is vision. When the heart is unobstructed, the result is love.

Twelve

Begin to Heal

How are we to find a solution for dissatisfaction in life? When our life is unsatisfactory we look for a solution. How do we find happiness, peace, and love for ourselves, or help someone to be happy? We don't need a book, scriptures, or religions. We don't need a guru or primitive rituals. We only need our five senses. Look at your body and your mind; they are all we need. There we will find everything we need, along with the resources that God gives us.

Our lives are so unsatisfactory! We have no peace, no pleasure; what we have is suffering. Without suffering, we would have love. The only reason we are not loving all the time is that we are suffering. If we didn't suffer, we would love.

We would be at peace, spreading love and peace all around us.

There is a reason for our suffering. That is Buddha's great insight. His genius was made manifest when he cried out that there is a reason for suffering and that if we were to discover it we could destroy it. We would have freedom, Nirvana.

What causes suffering? Mental activity, constructing our thoughts. Sometimes the mind is in repose, and all is well. But sometimes it begins to act, elaborating what Buddha calls the construction of thoughts. It begins to make judgments, evaluations, different and varied thoughts. The mind moves along in a way that means evaluating things and judging persons and events. Suffering is the result of evaluations, judgments, and mental constructs.

If the mind doesn't judge, there's no suffering, nor is there any emotion. Sheer joy is all there is. All of us at particular moments in our lives have already experienced this joy. Call it grace, coincidence, luck, or whatever you want. Suddenly we are filled with peace, the mind is no longer agitated, and we experience joy and pleasure.

If we don't understand how our minds work, we will begin to rely only on our mental constructions and we will be at the mercy of reason. We will base ourselves not on things, but on mental constructs. We will be imprisoned in what has been invented by the mind.

We walk down the street and hear beautiful music. We're carried away. Then the mental construct comes along: "What beautiful music; I'd like to hear it again. I'm going to buy a recorder, because I need this recording. I'll have to make an effort to get these things." All of it constructed by the mind.

Another person who might be passing by the same street could hear the same music and could also be carried away with it. But that person says, "I would like to hear this music again, but if I can't buy a recorder, I can make an equally rapturous music resound in my heart." Constructs of the mind create anxiety, disquietude. The music is magical, marvelous; I enjoy it. We're not at the

mercy of the music that we have heard or of the recorder; we're controlled by the assessments made by our minds.

What are your mind's normal judgments? Have you already heard statements from within like, "You shouldn't do this; you shouldn't speak about these things; you need this; you deserve such and such; it should be more so and so?" Have you likewise heard unpressured, free invitations for you to make a decision, or do you still hear "ought" at each desire? "Oughts" make decisions unnecessary, for there is so much pressure from society and there are so many laws for sticking to the conventional that the only thing we can do is to act in accordance with interior demands.

Do you realize that these "oughts" are signs of family ties that come from a distant past? They were marvelous in the past but now they aren't even real. They are souvenirs from our past, from where we have been, but they no longer bring us life. They hold neither love, nor affection, nor concern. They are a mental drug. They come from another place and time unrelated to our here

and now. They have nothing to do with "us." "Oughts" are lifeless and unreal.

We must understand the mind's constructs. What is going on inside us? Imagine a man with no sense of sight or hearing. He would be unable to see or hear and would be living in a world where all other persons would be blind and deaf. What kind of world would he be living in? Would he someday suspect that the things he touches, smells, and tastes have another dimension, that of sight? And what if you were to grow up disdaining your five senses, sticking rigidly to the interpretation and "oughts" of the authorities? You would very likely never be able to trust your senses, your common sense, your own self, but instead you would strive throughout your whole life for the approval of the authorities when you thought, acted, spoke, and felt. Indeed, some societies force people to confess when they speak, think, touch, or act differently from the way established by authority.

Some religions do the same thing.

Whenever there is a degree of order related to obedience and authorities, there will be a deep and diffuse risk just beneath that superficial security. Power creates fear, conformity, and confinement. "Oughts" of the system can separate people from their own grace, beauty, and love.

You are not yourself nor have you been yourself since your earliest infancy. Would you like to discover who you really are? Would you have enough courage to become yourself? That is exciting. You can love a particular feeling, thought, or action of this new you. But you cannot have anyone to judge it and look out for it over your shoulders. This new life begins with self-acceptance and self-love and with confidence in your senses, all of them, in all respects. It is a special and thorough acceptance. Are you ready?

Jungle lions look out! Here I come! At last — after everything I've been—without fear.

～～ We have five senses. Is it possible that we might have five more, and thus the tree of life might show us things that we never would have suspected? It is because we don't have these senses that our mind cannot even conceive of such possibilities. People born blind and deaf cannot conceive that the flowers they smell and touch could have color. It would never occur to them that such a thing might exist. In order to really live and be yourself you will need this special gift of feeling and thinking the unknown. Those who live for the "ought" have no thoughts of their own, but only derived pleasures and thoughts, like those who laugh only when the boss laughs. They experience a "justifying" feeling before the laugh. Approval makes them right. Many adults need permission to do the least little thing, express the least opinion, or have any pleasure in life. The permission that only a child would seek is reflected in adults when they struggle for the freedom to make decisions, share, speak, even feel.

Rising above your conditioning will be as difficult as using your five feelings for the first time. You will feel strange and lonely when you trust them instead of following your need for approval, but the pleasure that you will then feel will be beyond any description: the resurrection of your life.

What do I see when I look at life? There is no way to know. Are the five senses introducing some new information into reality? Does reality hold something special or are your senses creating something that does not belong to it, or only partly? We don't know. How are we to know whether the color green that I see actually exists? Suppose that every time that I see green you see red and call it green. We would think we are seeing the same thing but we would not be. We don't know how much our perception is responsible for what we see, but how sad it would be if we didn't have it for discovering life.

If we fear authority, we don't trust in ourselves. How can I say whether my feelings are mine, based on my own perception of reality, or whether they are feelings that come from authority? Do you think you can have a correct way of feeling? Are you aware of anyone who has established something like that? How often do you see, think, feel, and act out of "ought"?

Without getting beyond the ought level, we don't even scratch reality, we don't even suspect what it is. We merely achieve concepts and images of reality through the laws of etiquette and behavior. We still haven't tasted the true flavor, nor have we loved. "Lord, I can see." "My God, it's wonderful!"

If we suppose that our feelings are purely receptive, we have a problem, because in fact they are very selective. Our mind is like a sieve; we don't see reality, we can't see it; we can only see what is projected, preselected by the mind. I can't see you, only the idea that exists of you in my mind. This is why we see double. I see in you things that someone else doesn't see and vice versa. In other words, in order for me to see you, I have to place you in my mind, on its selective side, and perceive: How much of reality is there? Just as much as exists in our minds. Is that reality?

What subsists in the mind is constantly filtered. What are the filters? My fears, desires, relations, beliefs, habits, and conditioning. They select what is perceived by my senses. I don't have real sensations; I react to images formed in my mind. I can look at someone, see an American, and have a good feeling; someone else seeing the same person could have a feeling of repugnance. Is it a human being that is being seen? Or an image? In someone else's reaction we can see if that person is responding to the impulse of the here and now or to a preconceived image.

When you desire something, you are aware of many things that other persons don't notice. A mother can be sound asleep with jet planes roaring overhead, but at the first murmur from her baby she will wake up. Why? Her senses filter out other sounds. That also happens inside us. We have there a censor that acts on what we experience. Our perception depends on past conditioning.

Someone who feels inferior will constantly perceive things that confirm that belief. We are always confirming our beliefs. If I think something about Americans, I will see in them things that confirm what I think. So we live with so many things filtered, selected, censored. What actually is there in our minds? We add to our images mental constructs and evaluations: "This is good, this is bad, true, untrue, etc." Actually there is no good or evil in persons or in nature. There is only a mental judgment imposed on this or that reality: which team is good, which is best, when a victory is well earned, when the game isn't well played. In reality all that exists is a game and the people playing in it, a ball that is thrown, kicked, hurled. Ball and players move back and forth. People then add their particular evaluations to these actions in life; they cheer more for a uniform or for an idea than for the reality that is already there. They applaud their own conditioning and preferences much more than the reality they observe. Isn't that stupid?

We end up in this common confusion because we go running after things like idiots, not even knowing what they are. We keep adding our filters, evaluations, and desires to reality. We insert good and evil into reality as though we were filling a balloon; we say that things are desirable, undesirable, true, false. But things are what they are, whether we understand them or not.

〜〜〜 What is awareness? It is the capacity to observe when we are filtering reality, not just the persisting image. We must become aware:

The self has invented the notion of the ego, the I. If I look at the world, in my stupidity, I have projected the "mine" onto buildings, computers, cities, onto reality. Give me something and I am likely to project onto it something of my ego. This "mine" exists only in my head, because if I were to die tonight, nothing in that building would change. Things are what they are. They're not mine, yours, or someone else's. That is a mere convention among us.

Let us suppose a building is yours. Your possession of it, however, in a sense involves just a projection, one that can cause suffering. The building is a building. The root of all suffering is being attached, taking hold of. Being attached is nothing more than projecting the "ego," the "mine," onto something. As soon as you project the self onto something, attachment takes hold. When we slowly remove the terms "I," "me," and "mine" from our properties, buildings, clothing, society, country, religion, from our body, from our personality, the result is liberation, freedom, moksha. When there's no longer self, things are what they are. You let life be life.

Realize that everything is transitory, unsatisfactory, and void of self. Paradoxically, that is the secret formula for ongoing delight. Jesus realized this. "Who is my mother, my brother, my sister? I don't have any." There's a woman out there, but my mother is a concept in my mind. Relationships are a function, a projection, of my mind. No one wants to see this, so everybody is crazy, ill. We are living in a world we have created, thereby giving rise to both suffering and emotion; we are constantly seeking relief from the confusion they cause. It is as though after being cut, we sought to impose on ourselves the punishment of another cut. Endless confusion.

It is not just the "This is mine" that creates problems, but the "I am this, that, and the other thing." Identification with the "self" can cause problems. For example, "I am good, I am bad, I am an adorable person, I am impatient." My combination is different from yours. Your projections of my person aren't the same as mine. Nor are my projections of myself the same. Who you say I am is not what I am. Not even I can express in words what I am.

If the ego did not exist, there would be no evil. If the Sikhs didn't have a collective ego, there would be no problems. The same is true of Brazilians, Spaniards, Indians, or for any nationality or religion. All conventions, labels, and limits are invented in our mind. Fifty years ago there was no Pakistani ego; three centuries ago no one lived or died for something called the American ego. Ten centuries ago there was no Muslim ego; twenty centuries ago, there was no Christian ego. Such things are conventions that are not inherent in life; they weren't created by God in nature; they are made, defined, written down, out of people's ideas. Things are what they are. The ego is a creation of the mind.

Our minds create labels and apply them to individuals, saying that from now on this or that group is separate. Then we ask people to offer their lives for the defense of the labels we create. We call this something glorious like dying for the faith; actually they die for conventions, for concepts that don't exist in reality. These people are promised invisible rewards; for example, if you die for the faith, for your country, for God, you will have an eternal reward, even though it's not real. Concepts are superimposed, and reward itself is conceptual. Relearning to experience reality, to see it clearly, is a difficult path. Few are chosen. The mass mentality, the desire to be successful, and the ratification of the promises of the self are more seductive and often more attractive than real life. God help us!

~~~ So what is meditation? Meditation means observing everything found in the filters

of our consciousness, seeing, recognizing, being aware that everything is transitory, unsatisfactory, and free of self. One of the Buddhist masters said, "You can spend your whole life contemplating the tendency of your mind to label good and evil in all things." I assure you that if we could observe the work of our mind, we would never be bored for a minute. The mind creates good and evil all the time, sending messages in reaction to judgments. "This is good" (judgment) and so desirable (message); "this is bad, undesirable." This activity is going on all the time. It's wonderful to recognize that these actions are actually created by my mind. Good and evil do not exist in reality, nor does desirability or undesirability. This scene is our own invention. It is fascinating; it is as though we were going to play a computer game with the best players in the world. We would be training for the rest of our lives. We would never know a minute of boredom. We would enjoy our life because we would not take seriously all our wants or dislikes.

We need to resist what blemishes the mind, what corrupts the heart. "Blessed be the pure of heart, for they shall find God." When we can purify our hearts of all attachments and aversions, we will see God. Religion isn't a matter of rituals or academic studies. It isn't some sort of worship or good actions. Religion is about uprooting impurities from the heart. It is the path toward meeting God. When we have no antipathies or attachments, our love is reborn and grows. We will then know love. Otherwise, we will just be occupied with some images in our minds. No attachment, no aversion, just love; recognize this and you will accept in your heart what you want to be.

In religious terms, God is in control of all things; God's holy will is done whatever one's actions and thoughts; that is religion. Purify your heart, remove the impurities called attachments and aversions. Contemplate your mind's judgments of good and evil, and how they take over your being.

Those who have reached emptiness, a stage of nonjudgment, cease to be persons. They go through life, within life, brimming with life, and nothing has the power to destroy them. It is as though they threw ink at a wall and it didn't stick. The great master Hakwin left no disciples, writings, nothing. Of him it was said, "When he went into a forest not even a leaf was disturbed, when he went into the water, he made not the slightest wave; he didn't upset the harmony of the world."

Even an uproar will never disturb us. Things are what they are. The uproar exists in our heads, not in reality. It is our judgments that turn this uproar into a disturbance; other persons might not be disturbed because they would be able to reach different judgments.

Meditation is not attachment, identification, or owning. Such actions lead only to suffering. Meditation is observation. It leads to questioning and to love.

Thirteen

Dare to Feel

All psychological problems derive from inhibition. What is the difference between a normal person and a healthy person? The normal person lives by norms. A healthy person is like a barbarian. (If someone is happy, it shows, you know it, you feel it.) Such a person is healthy but doesn't fit into society. How can we keep our basic emotional health and also fit into society?

Life is based on emotion. The creatures that survive in the jungle are the ones that pounce and kill. The genteel inhibited person hides behind a tree and acts dead—internalizing fear. The human species would never have survived if it had been inhibited. Our ancestors were the bravest and most courageous of the species.

Personality isn't about logic and conformity; it's about feelings, especially those that are expressed and communicated. Many brilliant people are as opaque as dirty water. It is their emotional training that determines whether they are of the healthy or inhibited type. Children are genuine because they are emotionally open. A naive childhood is a happy childhood. If children or adolescents do not have permission to act as what they are, they are destined to act like children when they grow up. A baby is born free but its parents then chain it up. Sometimes the child never becomes free.

Are you chained up tight?

〜〜 The tragedy in this play is that all the villains are disguised as friends. Authority seems so interested and well intentioned when it teaches conformity and manipulates people's education. Men apparently have more psychological problems than women. Look at those who stutter, for example. There are ten men who stutter for every woman. The degree of stress and tension is the same, but relief varies a great deal. Women apparently have permission from society to express their feelings more. They can cry more easily. They speak the language of feelings more easily. Men don't, and we pay the price.

Have you noticed that when people are drinking their feelings flow, and for a short time their emotional problems are relieved? The person becomes uninhibited. Alcohol is a chemical that temporarily frees the emotions. A temporary relief, however, is by no means a solution for inhibitions.

Emotion is the basic rule of life. Inhibit someone's natural feelings, and neuroses are going to break out. All animals need sensory stimulation. There's no such thing as a neurotic animal in nature. But if an animal in a laboratory is deprived of sensory stimulation, touch, smell, taste, and so forth, it becomes depressed or hyperactive.

Around 85 percent of members of religious orders are depressed, because they have many duties, countless ideals, and not enough sensory stimulation. They also become depressed or hyperactive. Staying active is one kind of stimulation, but people also need emotional stimuli.

How do people receive emotional stimuli? By expressing their emotions. When you are physically inactive, give yourself some stimulus by walking or exercising. When you are depressed, take a risk emotionally. That way your emotions will go back to flowing normally. When the emotional and sensory stimuli are blocked inside us, we become depressed. Express your feelings. Look how easily children — unreligious, fearless, unrepressed — do it. You won't need others to stimulate you emotionally. You will be the center; you will not be hiding behind the tree. You will express your feelings, not paying too much attention to whether other people respond to them or not.

Why be so dependent on what others think? Why let yourself be inhibited? As your emotions flow, you won't need others, nor will you fear their opinions, stated or unstated. There will be so much grace and richness within you, and there will be so much life and emotion available to you at any time, that you will wonder whether you really need people. Once your fear of a particular person is gone, you will be free. You may want to examine whether you have transferred that fear to some other person. We easily replace desires, dependencies, and fears. If that's the case, you will have to free yourself of them as well. The vice of approval is deep and quickly takes root. Your inhibitions were simply fears. How can you have been so irascible, hateful, even fearful of these persons that you claimed to love? Because you wanted something that you thought was necessary for surviving emotionally, and you wanted it from them. It is impossible to love in the midst of fear or despair. Do you still want something from them? The choice is: love or desiring something; being free or wanting others to change.

If children were not intimidated, they would always be fine. They can hear, learn, and observe, but why compound their experience and mistakes with fear, shame, evil, and sin? Where do we learn this? Do you remember who taught you shame and fear as values?

"That's no way to behave in front of a guest."

"Sorry, mommy."

"Apologize to him."

"I'm sorry."

"I'm ashamed of you; I hope you have a bit of shame on your face" — and so forth.

Mistakes are normal and healthy; if there are no mistakes, there won't be any risks, just calculated conformity. That isn't life or the meaning of creation or the experience of love or the gospel message.

~~~ What sort of an explanation do you have for why someone lives in conformity? Fear personified? Emotional abuse is usually masked as teaching, family ties, authority, and obedience. What are children learning? Do you get worried when you make a mistake or disappoint others? Are you afraid of being chastised or disapproved of? You are a rare specimen even in the anguish

of your conditioning. Are you aware of how much you are striving to live in accordance with the expectations of others?

Who has taught you to express yourself, to live free and happy? On the other hand, who has taught you that the path to happiness was approval and acceptance by society?

Think about your happiest moments. What were you doing? You will recall that you spoke without thinking about what others might think. You acted freely and confidently. You were not interested in pleasing.

We have been trained to be unhappy. We have been told, "Think first, then speak." We have been trained to be specialists in winning approval, in censoring everything: "Think twice before you speak; don't express your feelings; say what other people expect; think about what other people may be thinking." And everyone begins to say what other people may be thinking. Do any of us manage to express ourselves in real life?

~~~ We have lived in keeping with an awareness censor, an authority, and a fuzzy and paranoid idea of "other people." Could you define your happiness as an effort to be accepted by the vague notion of "other people"? Some members of religious congregations have been so repressed that they have spent a lifetime of unhappiness trying to win the approval of a concept, the concept of "God." And they remain emotionally needy forever, and thanks to this concept, also spiritually needy. The proportion is very large, around 85 percent.

People ask, "How have I become so inhibited, full of fear, incapable of expressing my feelings?" They really mean, "How was the natural emotion of my childhood taken away from me?" When, by whom, and how has this emotional component been twisted and distorted? At this point it doesn't much matter where the process began. What's needed is to heal the person. What began in which person or with which event is unimportant. Heal the person. The past is dead, buried, and risen. Goodness and evil come from it. Life comes from it. Let's love the past. Let's also heal the present, precisely in the situation of the now, which is crucial for life. That will be enough.

Inhibited and selfish people are always preoccupied with themselves. They don't like themselves; they become unattractive because they don't reveal their feelings and they hide their gifts; they don't accept their portion of risk along with others. They devote little thought to others; they have no ability to look outside themselves, toward those around them. They have learned to live for approval, and there is never enough of it. Inhibited people don't love even while wanting to be loved. There is no love without involvement. They remain enclosed in their shells.

Everyone has problems, but if they express themselves the problems go away; such people don't need therapy.

A client says to the therapist: "I'm passionate about you."

Therapist: "You are?"

Client: "Yes, I feel very much in love with you."

Therapist: "Great! And how do you feel?"

Client: "I enjoy thinking about you, imagining myself talking with you. I'm happy when I leave our sessions. I feel good sharing my feelings with you. Can we continue the therapy now?"

Therapist: "Don't you want to know what I think about all this?"

Client: "No."

How delightful! It's wonderful, being able to express feelings freely, unimpeded, to express our feelings to someone who understands.

All psychological problems are the result of our inability to express our feelings. We're frightened. We don't know how to express feelings, either negative or positive. We are illiterates in expressing feelings. We're afraid. We can speak about our problems, but not about feelings.

Carl Rogers talks about congruence. Congruence is revealing my problem to you; it's risky. It means being willing to share with you my feeling about you and about the situation. I can say, "I'm passionate about you; I'm fascinated; I find you sexually attractive; but there's something in you that I don't like; sometimes I'm very annoyed with you," and so forth. Yet we almost never say these things that reveal us and illuminate our mystery. "There's something in you that affects me and has a deep influence on me. I'm not sure what that means." Feelings are very close to my inner self. What would happen if people were to know not what I've done, but what I am and what I'm feeling?

The inhibited person suffers from emotional constipation. Being in good physical condition requires internal generation, that is, that nutrients generate energy and what's left be discarded. Nutrients have to pass through the body regularly. Likewise, the generation of feelings requires continual discharging. We must let it flow. Otherwise the psychological buildup is poisonous, and the ulcer makes its insidious appearance. It's because of our good manners, the etiquette and approval of society, that we all contribute toward this internal constipation and that emotional hypocrisy builds up. Such people have no feelings or desire or joy in being alive. Some people find it difficult to get up in the morning; others feel nervous when they have to meet people. Facing the world head on demands emotion in order to leave behind the safety and confinement of the womb and to shift from a way of life consisting of darkness and immobility to one of risk and flow. In striving to keep safe and removed from risk to life, the core of the inhibiting personality suppresses the will, all energy turns inward, and the flow of life is blocked.

Inhibited people are both very selfish because they are self-absorbed, and yet not selfish enough, because they don't struggle on their own behalf. They live in an ivory tower, even though they insist they are quite sensitive to their surroundings. Inhibited people are always trying to please. They're sitting on the fence; they can be expressive or calm about everything except what they feel. They have a hard time saying no because they continually need affirmation. They think that by saying yes they can get what they are striving for. They're tense. They don't know how to relax. They're indecisive and secretive. They wouldn't tell you what they had for lunch. They avoid the word "I."

Have you noticed how people who display good manners seem to be overly inhibited? But the uninhibited aren't necessarily those who have been poorly brought up. Whether the problem is dependency on drugs or sex, a compulsive need for approval, or even more obvious problems like stuttering or shyness, they have been caused in childhood by inhibition. Uninhibitedness can be brought about. People can be healed. Just speak, always speak, with feeling. That's what children do all day long (until they start going to school). They show their feelings to others, to some people in particular, to nannies, teddy bears, friends (unless they are inhibited). That is what intimacy is about. That's what love is about. And that is what the world needs most.

Part Two

*Religion isn't a matter of rituals or
academic studies. It isn't some sort of
worship or good actions. Religion is
about uprooting impurities from the heart.
It is the path toward meeting God.*

Fourteen

18 Exercises

Exercise A ～～

Uncover the fears and anxieties in your relationships.

1. Choose one of them.

2. Behind each anxiety lies a demand that you have made. Can you clearly pick out that demand?

3. Become aware of the expectation or source of that demand. (There must be something that has led you to believe in a particular idea. For example, the belief that others are necessary for your happiness, or that other people's behavior can create or control your happiness.)

4. Now look within yourself, and realize that there is a wide realm of self-sufficient happiness. You failed to find it within yourself previously because your attention was focused on the things you believed in or on your illusions about the world. When we are happy, anxieties disappear.

For consideration:

Desire is certainly not love, although it is continually being confused with it. In a frenetic striving for gratification, desire leaves its home, its core, endlessly looking for something more. Love is already there at home, within you.

Exercise B ∼∼

1. Think about things that you have been fighting or struggling to get.

2. Become aware that you have no need for most of these things.

3. Imagine for a moment that you have lost your fear of living without such things.

4. Imagine that you have lost the fear of being a nobody.

5. Nourish this courageous feeling. You have attained happiness. Can you feel it? Happiness lies not in what the self has, but in what the self is. Your self is already what it needs to be. Can you see that? That is true faith.

18 Exercises

For consideration:

Life is too important to be wasted in yearning to be rich, famous, good looking, popular, or pretty, or in dreading being poor, unknown, ignored, or ugly. These things become unimportant, as though they were pebbles alongside a dazzling diamond. You—your true self—have always been and will always be a diamond. Your life is priceless. Would you use a precious manuscript to light a fire? The need to impress is a waste of your precious life. It is attitudes like these that cause most of the unhappiness in the world. Be real, not make-believe.

Exercise C 〰️

1. Think about people who praise you. What do they say? Tell yourself: "These praises are not my self; they belong to my self." Don't identify yourself with things, ideas, words, or labels. If necessary, establish merely a distant association.

2. Think about people who criticize you. What do they say? Say to yourself, "These criticisms are not my self; they refer to me." The only thing that exists is a distant association. Don't be identified with things, ideas, words, or labels.

3. Think about how you have blamed yourself for some past mistake. Say to yourself, "These reproofs are not my self; they are distantly related to me. My ideas and my judgments are not my self. They may be mine, but they're not me." The self is not bad or good, it's not pretty or ugly, smart or stupid. It simply is. Indescribable, like spirit. All things—like your feelings,

thoughts, and cells—come and go. Don't be identified with any of them. The self is not any of them.

For consideration:

There's no need to try. Spirituality is actually a matter of who we are, of becoming what we are, of seeing who we are. Even though we may have acted honestly, vainly, insanely, unjustifiably, or cruelly, we are saved by realizing what we have not realized thus far. When we discover that our essence is unique and unchangeable, that our self is what it has always been by God's grace, we arrive at our spiritual self. We don't have to attempt to perceive the Good News. We have a diamond mine within us; we are the Reign. You will realize that you are finally free when you no longer have a childish need to be "right." You will not be desperate for air, life, or God once you have attained the awareness that you already possess them.

Exercise D ～～

1. Make a list of things that normally disturb you.

2. Become aware that as hard to believe as it may seem, nothing, absolutely nothing, has the power to disturb you. All disturbance comes from attachment to the illusion of "identification," which means that you are under the impression that this illusion is your self. When we are aware, no human injustice or evil has the power to disturb us. No matter what happens we are at peace. An out-of-control car cannot run over someone who is in a plane. The darkest clouds don't disturb the sky.

3. Now go back to that list and say, "I am not this or that. No matter what happens, I am not going to lose my true self." No one will be able to keep your self from you and say, "Jump, submit, obey, and I'll give you your own self." You no longer think

someone else has power to give you your own self, or to take it. Do you know what it means to no longer feel disgusted or resentful? This is a priceless pearl. What do you intend to give in return?

For consideration:

There is no need to be popular. No need to be loved or accepted. No need to stand out or be important. These are not basic human needs. They are desires that arise from the ego—the conditioned self—from the me. Something deep down inside you, your self, has no interest in such things. It already has all it needs to be happy. All that you need is to be aware of your attachments, of the illusions that these things are, and you will be on the way to freedom.

Exercise E ~~~

1. If you are seeking to be happy, strive not to fulfill your desires, for they are not answers for your life. To be happy, give up your desires, or transform them by understanding their limited value. Fulfillment of desires brings relief and comfort, not happiness.

2. Think about things you desire intensely. Examine them one by one and ask, "Could I be happy whether these desires were realized or not? Wouldn't it be wonderful?"

3. Realize that there are thousands of people truly happy without those things or persons that you so ardently desire.

4. Now tell each of these desired things or persons, "I sincerely want to be happy without you, because you aren't my happiness." You can't let yourself live with

false identifications; go on to admit that they are nothing but personal preferences.

For consideration:

There is no natural human impulse to be important, to be somehow more than others, or to be considered greater than others. Desires to be popular, successful, or even loved are created needs. The only natural impulse that exists is to be free, free from the burdensome desire to be important, successful, popular, or loved. Being free from the need to be rewarded and applauded is the freedom worthy of our stature as children of God.

Exercise F 〰〰

1. Observe your disappointment when something does not happen the way you wanted, someone doesn't treat you the way you expected, or you are laid low by some criticism. Understand what causes this sharp reaction within you, or why you are so dismayed at the criticism or what has happened.

2. Become aware of your feelings of shame and guilt from the deceptions of the past. Do you realize how you are capable of judging yourself and causing negative feelings and unhappiness? See how much self-compassion there is for your griefs. Realize that it is only you condemning yourself, apologize to yourself, and let yourself be enlightened. What a revelation! Every least bit of suffering, every negative emotion can lead you to understanding, clarity, happiness, and freedom if you know how to use them, to allow yourself

time to understand, as though you were barely able to see. Lord, that I may see. Understanding: the secret of a happy life.

For consideration:

Pleasant experiences make life pleasurable; painful experiences lead to growth. Suffering shows us where we are not well, where we are not yet growing, just as painful points are symptoms of specific illness or of parts of the body that are overloaded. Don't waste any suffering that falls upon you.

Exercise G

1. Stand in front of a friend and say: "I leave you free to be yourself, to have your own thoughts, to follow your inclinations, to surrender to your predilections, to live your life the way you want. I'm not going to make demands; I don't want you to be the way I desire. I'm not going to nourish expectations about what you ought to be or do in the future."

2. Also say, "From now on, I'm going to be free to have my own thoughts to follow, to surrender to, to live my life the way I want."

3. If you can't bring yourself to say these words, what does that say about you? About the nature of your friendships? About the quality of your life?

18 Exercises

For consideration:

Never do favors so people will be grateful to you. They will recognize your yearning for thanks or praise and feel that they are being obliged to do something, if not being manipulated. Some acts encourage the false belief that your strength is more in others than in yourself. Idolatry is an illusion that sees greater power in outside forces than within us. When you give someone power over you, you are creating an idol.

Exercise H 〜

1. Look at people whom you know and like. See them as selfish, and then as foolish. Think of times when they might be immature and small-minded, then fearful and confused, and finally, innocent and blameless.

2. Look at people whom you admire, about whom you have read, to whom you have prayed, Jesus for example. See them as selfish, immature, and small-minded, fearful and confused, innocent, blameless.

3. Think about yourself. See yourself as foolish, selfish, small-minded, confused, ignorant, innocent, blameless.

4. Are there some characteristics that you would not be able to accept and would not be willing to apply to yourself or to them? Would you be disappointed if what was said about them and about you were true? Do you love them all the more for their limitations and weaknesses? Can you

accept them as simply human? Accept them as persons who can be loved? Can you see how God could love all the idiosyncrasies of all people, along with their imperfections and virtues?

For consideration:

You are never passionate about someone. You become impassioned over the hopeful ideas and pleasant feelings that you create about someone. You never trust anyone; you simply trust in your judgment about the person. When your judgment about a person changes, your trust also changes.

Exercise I 〜〜

1. Think about all the controls to which you have submitted due to your need for company and the approval of other people. You have waived your freedom for the sake of accommodation. Why did you do it? Can you tell us what you gained in so doing?

2. Let people come and go as though they didn't make any difference to you. The most beautiful redemption and liberation and freedom are experienced when you let other people alone, being, loving, and growing, and not imposing, interfering, and shaping their lives. Now perceive how interference and static diminish as soon as you stop pretending to be interested and concerned. Actually, it doesn't make any difference. Aren't they being liberated? Aren't you being liberated? Do you see the demands, expectations, and virtues that you have relinquished?

3. This is not insensitivity; it is love. It is indifference, acceptance, and affection of the highest order. But don't expect people to understand such a thing. Don't suppose that people will have eyes to see. They have been programmed to judge others and themselves in accordance with patterns from the past, social conventions, and religious beliefs.

For consideration:

The main reason for the world's sadness is simply the inability of human beings to not let themselves be deceived by dissembling learned from other people. Is someone interested in you for what he or she can get or wants from you? That's normal. Is someone insisting that you live your life in accordance with their own pleasure or to satisfy their desires? Family or friends? Is someone insisting that you live your life according to the rules that some other person has established? Your parents or authorities? What kind of person tries to control others? Are you allowing someone to hypocritically force you to have feelings of selfishness and ingratitude? How can someone do that? Are you determined to disappoint such demands and the persons who want you to do things their way?

Exercise J

1. Imagine that you have come to a stage where you do not feel the need to offer anyone explanations about yourself. What does it feel like not to have to justify your actions, ask permission, or offer excuses? How do you behave? Do you think you will be able to reach this stage in the near future?

2. Imagine that you have no need to impress anyone. How do you feel? How do you act when you are not trying to impress? What do you think you would need to do to reach that stage?

3. The most wearisome slavery in the world is worrying: "What sort of impression am I making on others?" It pushes people to try to look intelligent, charming, generous, etc. Do you know someone who is like that? How do you feel toward that person? Can you realize that a president or a pope who acted like that would really be a slave?

For consideration:

Paraphrasing George Santayana, "Humans are gregarious animals far more in their thoughts than in their body. They can enjoy going out alone for a walk, but they hate to be alone in their opinions." The first thing that education ought to give a person is the ability to be alone and the courage to trust in his or her own eyes, mind and heart, observations, thoughts, and feelings. Do you agree?

Exercise K 〜〜〜

1. Think about someone to whom you are attached. Tell that person, "I don't see you as you are, but as I imagine you to be."

2. Think about someone you don't like. Say, "I don't see you as you are, but as I imagine you to be."

3. Once you have attained awareness and love, before long you will not be liking or disliking in the ordinary sense of the word.

4. It is wonderful to realize that my vision and imagination are mine and belong to me. It is wonderful to comprehend that the reality that I see simply is, and that others simply are who they are. I am never going to be able to understand them or possess their reality.

For consideration:

It is not selfishness to live as you see fit. Selfishness is insisting that other people live as you see fit. Do you know someone who is selfish? What position in life does he or she hold? And is that a good place for a selfish person? Does it affect that person somehow? Can you remember a time when you demanded that someone else live by your demands, or when you insisted that everyone live the way you see fit? Authority is, with rare exceptions, selfish.

Exercise L ～～

1. Think about some disagreeable experience that you have had with another person.

2. Think about it as a golden opportunity.

   • See the person as he or she is, not as idealized by you. To have expectations is to idealize.

   • Grow in self-knowledge.

   • Accept the other as he or she is, without condemnation or judgment.

3. See in the other person's inappropriate behavior a cry for help. That person is a captive of his or her mental machinations; captive to his or her programming, just like you in the past. He or she is unable to escape from illusion.

18 Exercises

For consideration:

It is an illusion to think that someone can do good to others, organize effective movements for a "better world," or do away with evil. Take off your blindfold. Only by becoming personally aware can someone develop. Social schemes that seek vast improvements or the protection of others often do great damage. What difference is there between a freedom fighter and a terrorist? What difference is there between a KGB spy and one from the CIA, between Chile's DINA and Israel's Mossad? Who are they protecting, and who are they destroying? Violence brings greater violence. People who are ill from drinking contaminated water are not going to be cured by drinking more of that same water. The remedy is poisoned with violence, with self-centeredness. Let people be. Let yourself be. Live your life and stop interfering.

Exercise M ~~~

Here is a path toward a new perception and consciousness.

1. Think about something that a person has said or done.

2. Now ignore the action and the words and look beyond the surface of the facts.

3. Understand the real, inner reason. Isn't it gratifying to see with the heart and the mind instead of being literal or letting yourself be swayed by prejudice?

For consideration:

There is a Chinese saying that goes: "There is nothing so cruel as nature. In the whole universe there's no escaping it. But it is not nature that attacks; it is the heart of human beings."

18 Exercises

Exercise N 〰️

Here are some steps for arriving at a higher level where love is experienced, where you don't let yourself be bewitched, affected negatively, or wounded by others. This exercise will help you overcome the emptiness of rejection and the absolute uselessness and superficiality of approval by others. You will be able to make allowances, to do away with self-praise or self-condemnation, once their irrelevance has been established.

1. Think about someone whose approval you desire. Realize that in the presence of that person you lose the freedom to be yourself and accept that person as he or she is, because of your need for that person.

2. When you are alone, what kind of presence do you need? Think about someone whose presence is absolutely necessary to enable you to put aside your feeling of not being well. See that in the presence of this person you are not free, because you regard him or her as necessary for your happiness.

3. Think about persons on whom you have conferred the power to make you happy or miserable.

4. Don't let yourself be deceived by illusion. You don't need anyone as an emotional crutch. As soon as you become aware of this, no one will ever have power over you. Your emotional highs and lows will be over. You will go on to be your own master in your relations with others. You will not be at the mercy of anyone. Now you are free. You can love. Your spirituality and your humanity have been restored.

For consideration:

Taking care of yourself is a selfish and self-sufficient attitude but it is Christian in its origins and healthy in its results. Learn to live fully, humanly, and happily day by day. The truly human approach is to learn to swim and not be drowned with your friend.

18 Exercises

Exercise O 〜〜

1. Say to a friend, "I know that in the things that are really important I can't rely on you. I can't make you my support, because you are powerless to help me."

2. Realize how fascinating it is to be without a single friend or adviser you can rely on. When you see the inability of others to help you, you discover the Reign within you.

3. Realize how wonderful it is to be free of illusions about your best friends, not out of cynicism or injury, but because you are aware of reality. For they are powerless to help you in the things that really matter. Recall the seemingly harsh words of Jesus about relatives. What could Peter, James, or John do for Jesus on Holy Thursday, or Good Friday, or any other time? Being freed of illusions brings a glorious opportunity. It is like awakening to a new life. You are okay, even when you think you aren't.

For consideration:

People who are aware enjoy everything. If you ask them why, they will reply, "Why not?" The aware person lives in a world of the self (the not-self), where loneliness and unhappiness are impossible, inconceivable. The aware person lives in a world of uniqueness and variety, of renewal and the now.

Exercise P

1. Imagine a future world where no one has any more power to hurt. Where business people are no longer engaged in combat, competition is not to the death, women aren't afraid of their husbands, children and parents don't threaten each other. Where people don't nourish feelings of anxiety, and those who live alone don't feel lonely. Where citizens are not terrorized by a dominating government. Where no one is afraid of anyone.

2. Barring a miracle, is it possible to come to live like that?

3. How? Why don't you start making such a world a reality?

Exercise Q 〜〜

Are you unhappy with the people in your life? Do you find them ungrateful, untrustworthy, contemptible, selfish, or temperamental?

1. Here is a miraculous, infallible route toward changing them (at least in relationship to you).

  • Change yourself. When you change, then they will change. The problem is not entirely in them, but rather in the way you interact with them.

  • The problem lies in the demands and expectations that you have toward them. Cease that, and see what happens.

- Tell each of them, "I have no right to demand or expect something from you."

2. When someone demands something of you that you detest, you have a strong desire for them to change or to stop acting that way. In that situation, think about the following:

- Can you see that you are expecting that person to change instead of changing and growing yourself?

- That person is very probably waiting for you to change first.

- Thus a chasm is going to grow between you, and this relationship may continue to be painful for years, each waiting for the other to change or die.

18 Exercises

For consideration:

Which is more accurate: I feel good because the world is good? Or the world is good because I feel good?

Exercise R ～～

Think about some suffering, abhorrence, or concern that you have had. Now realize that had you had a greater understanding, you would not have felt pain.

Fifteen
Reminders

1. Our happiness or unhappiness depends more on the way we perceive and deal with events than on their nature in themselves. If you are not enjoying your life, there is something radically wrong with you.

2. Do you live by the Spirit or by the Law? The authorities want to make you believe that if you haven't obeyed the laws during this past hour, you've wasted it. The ambitious want to make you believe that if you haven't produced during this past hour, you've wasted it. The Spirit inspires you to believe, "If you haven't taken advantage of this past hour, you have gained it."

3. An angel appears to you and says, "You can have anything you want." What would you ask for? Why?

4. Do not feel ashamed of anything that you have done in the past.

5. All the barriers preventing us from attaining happiness are self-imposed. Are you aware that for all these years you have been responsible for your own happiness? Have you let yourself be controlled by another person for some time? What false belief led you to do that?

6. It is not how much we have but rather how much we enjoy that makes us happy. We can enjoy life only when we are not afraid of loss. And we become free when we finally become aware that what we know cannot be taken away or stolen from us, neither by others nor by ourselves.

7. If we really want to, we can be happy immediately, because happiness is in the present moment. Yet if we want to be happier than we are or happier than others, we then have the attributes of an unhappy person, because happinesses cannot be compared. Such a desire is insatiable. We can only be as happy as we are, and we cannot measure how happy others are.

8. Establishing relationships is possible only between people who are aware. People who are unaware cannot share love. They can only exchange desires, demands, mutual flattery, and manipulation. Test your love to see whether it is aware: when your particular desire is objected to or denied by the person loved, how quickly does your attachment become resentment?

9. The only devil is unawareness, which means the inability, ignorance, or failure to see life as it really is, to understand people as they are, and to accept others without fear. Looking at life more through belief systems than through the heart, eyes, and thinking is what is wrong with the world—unawareness. People are almost always ignorant of what they are doing. Most live a good part of their lives in unawareness, with mistaken identities.

10. The difference between us and criminals lies more in what we do than in what we are. Under the right set of circumstances, any behavior is possible.

11. There are no problems with other people. The only problem lies inside you. It's not other people who are the problem but how you react to them. Discover why you react in a particular way. That way you will be able to break with your illusions.

12. The only reason for your suffering is your ideas about how people ought to behave toward you, in the belief that your ideas are more correct. You are not suffering because of what others do, but from the expectation that they will behave as you wish. And they frustrate your expectations. It is your expectations that are hurting you. Lower your anxiety level and three wonderful things will happen:

• you will be at peace;

• people will keep acting in accordance with their own programming, and that will not cause you to suffer in the least;

• you will have more energy to do what you want, for you will not be wasting your time waiting for others to live according to the plans that you have drawn up for them.

13. Why are human relationships (friendship, dialogue, sex, etc.) so painful, so stressful, and so prone to cause anxiety? All suffering comes from unconscious expectations, demands, hopes, and desires. You want people to act the way you like. If you give up your expectations, the suffering will go away. You will experience a fantastic relief; it is like breathing pure air.

14. Love is not a relationship. It is a state of being. Are you in a state of love? Are you living it?

15. Perfect love casts out fear because it has no desires or demands, does not bargain, does not judge. Love simply is, it is present, it sees and acts.

16. What people often call "love" is actually self-interest. And once they learn to describe this love in terms of virtue and to live it in a way that is acceptable to others,

they think that their work is purely a service of loving apostolic dedication. But it remains self-interest camouflaged as generosity.

17. Loving people means being completely happy even without them, without fear of injury, without a concern to impress, without dreading that they might not like you any more or abandon you. No matter what they say or do, you remain at peace. Don't fill your emptiness with people and call it love.

18. The more you love others, the more you can do without them. The more you love others, the more you can do with them.

19. The best examination of conscience that you can perform is to ask, "How have I lived the past hour?"

Of Related Interest

Paula D'Arcy
THE GIFT OF THE RED BIRD
A Spiritual Encounter

When Paula D'Arcy lost her husband and baby in a car crash, she began an inner search for a faith that was stronger than fear. In *Gift of the Red Bird* she shares her remarkable spiritual adventure: Paula literally journeyed alone into the wilderness for three days, allowing the Creator to speak through that creation. As she surrendered to the power of God alone, a red bird appeared and, without words, began to teach...

"It is all a matter of seeing, but we need seers to show us how. Paula D'Arcy shatters our poor sight and shows us light."
—Richard Rohr

0-8245-1956-6, paperback

crossroad

Of Related Interest

Kenneth Leong
THE ZEN TEACHINGS OF JESUS

"I left Jesus to search for the Tao when I was sixteen," writes Kenneth Leong. "Now I am forty and realize that I could have found the Tao in Jesus." It is the spiritual side of Zen, the art of trusting and accepting life that coincides with the core of the Gospel message. Sometimes people have overlooked the joy, the humor, and the depth of Jesus' teachings — often because they could not surmount the narrow confines of openness to the scripture's power to transform our lives.

"In *The Zen Teachings of Jesus,* Kenneth S. Leong presents Jesus as poetic teacher of everyday wisdom, a sage who brings joy and fun to the way we see the world."
— Philip Endean, S.J., Heythrop College, editor of *The Way*

0-8245-1883-7, paperback

crossroad

Also by Anthony de Mello

PRAYING BODY AND SOUL

This book offers an intimate retreat with Anthony de Mello, who was a master-teacher of both the Eastern ways of meditation and the Western traditions of prayer, especially the Ignatian Exercises. Little step by little step, he leads us into the life-changing practices of prayer — prayer that includes the body, the mind, and the soul, our own experiences, the experiences of the people of God as reflected in the Holy Scriptures, and the teachings of the Church.

0-8245-1673-7, paperback

Check your local bookstore for availability.
To order directly from the publisher,
please call 1-800-707-0670 for Customer Service
or visit our Web site at *www.cpcbooks.com*.
For catalog orders,
please send your request to the address below.

THE CROSSROAD PUBLISHING COMPANY
16 Penn Plaza, Suite 1550
New York, NY 10001

crossroad